"GENTLEMEN, BE SEATED!"
A PARADE OF THE AMERICAN MINSTRELS

A CYCLE OF MINSTRELSY, FROM CABIN AND RIVER BOTTOM TO THE STAGE

"GENTLEMEN, BE SEATED!"

A PARADE OF THE AMERICAN MINSTRELS

By
DAILEY PASKMAN

REVISED EDITION

*Profusely Illustrated
from old prints and photographs
and with complete music
for voice and piano*

Clarkson N. Potter, Inc./Publisher NEW YORK

DISTRIBUTED BY CROWN PUBLISHERS, INC.

Library of Congress Cataloging in Publication Data
Paskman, Dailey.
    "Gentlemen, be seated!"

    Includes index.
    1. Minstrel shows—History. 2. Ballads,
American. I. Title.
PN3195.P3 1976   791.1'2   76-10702
ISBN 0-517-52587-9

DEDICATION

To all the lovers of minstrelsy, whether in the romantic setting of the past or the practical possibilities of the present, to the thousands who cherish an old song and even an old joke in a new interpretation, and to the great American public to whom the authentic materials of their own national background are of constantly increasing interest, this book is faithfully dedicated.

ACKNOWLEDGMENTS

So MANY people have been in some measure responsible for this book that it is impossible to make complete acknowledgment of the indebtedness of the author. In a few cases, however, a special word of appreciation can and must be given.

First and foremost comes a great debt of gratitude to Albert Davis, who has devoted most of his life to the collection of rare Americana, particularly in the field of minstrelsy, and who has generously contributed a large percentage of the pictures and music in this volume, besides putting at the disposal of the author a treasure-house of old playbills, manuscripts, and other original data, which provided much information not otherwise available.

J. P. Wilson, whose career has been closely identified with minstrelsy and theatricals in general, deserves hearty thanks for his valuable assistance in gathering authentic material.

Permission to use copyrighted material has been kindly given by M. Witmark & Sons, the Edward B. Marks Music Company, and the Oliver Ditson Company.

Colonel E. H. R. Green—son of the fabulous lady of her day, Hetty Green—should be mentioned gratefully for his unfailing encouragement and interest in the revival of minstrelsy, and thanks are extended also to the thousands of radio fans and theatre patrons whose enthusiasm fired the spark that eventually produced a burnt-cork conflagration.

Grateful acknowledgment is given to the New York Public Library and Museum of the Performing Arts at Lincoln Center, the Music and Theatre Departments; to Vera Brodsky Lawrence, whose collected works of Scott Joplin was published by the New York Public Library; to *The New York Times* and *The New York Daily News;* to Metro-Goldwyn-Mayer; to ASCAP; to Macmillan Publishing Company, Inc., publisher of *Nobody*, the story of Bert Williams, by Ann Charters, and to Alfred Fruch, whose cover art is reproduced here, and to Emerson-Loew for the photographs of Ben Vereen.

Special thanks to Patricia Horan for her editorial assistance in the production of this new edition.

AUTHOR'S NOTE

Since my early days in the theatre, I have been an incurable collector of memorabilia and material of the great minstrel performers. The homely and emotional songs and comedy sketches of these entertainers have always stirred my keen sense of pleasure.

When radio was in its infancy, and static was its infant cry, I was appointed Director of one of the first radio stations (WGBS) in New York. It was on this radio station that I had prepared and produced the first Minstrel Show on the air, "Dailey Paskman's Radio Minstrels." It was a tremendous popular success. It continued weekly for several years. The listening audiences kept sending me all kinds of out-of-print songs and minstrel data, which added greatly to my collection. Later this show went on the road to play the deluxe vaudeville theatres throughout the United States. Its popularity was such that phonograph records were made of it on Columbia Records and on Longines' "Memories of Radio" series.

During the reign of MGM's great musicals, Metro-Goldwyn-Mayer acquired the motion picture rights to my book, "*Gentlemen, Be Seated!*" and a portion of my book inspired a sequence in one of Arthur Freed's spectacular motion pictures, with Judy Garland and Mickey Rooney. It was truly a magnificent production of the minstrel "First Part"—an ensemble of hundreds of dancers, singers, and, of course, including the End Men and the pompous Interlocutor. The sequence scene is in the *new* MGM motion picture, *That's Entertainment.*

I have cherished memories of my association with George Gershwin, who was a close friend and with whom our mutual interest in Ragtime and Jazz music was a topic of great enjoyment. Our exchange of thoughts and material brought us a warm appreciation for those whose talent and creativity was to become a standard in the annals of music and homespun literary culture.

This book, then, has been written and compiled for lovers of the art of minstrelsy; for those who love the singing of a good song, and those who have made those songs famous, and for those who enjoy a funny joke, a lively bit of banter, and, above all, for those who delight in sharing the joy of mirth, stories, and melody in the good of happy fellowship.

These memorable days are not to be forgotten, but to be relived in the mind, in spirit.

DAILEY PASKMAN

New York, N.Y.

TABLE OF CONTENTS

LIST OF HALF-TONE ILLUSTRATIONS

"GENTLEMEN, BE SEATED!"
A PARADE OF THE AMERICAN MINSTRELS

THE SPIRIT OF MINSTRELSY

I. INTRODUCTORY

IT IS typical of our own United States that the most distinctive form of native entertainment should bear a name charged with all the romance and glamour of mediæval minstrelsy. We have applied the name of "ballad" to every sentimental song, regardless of its narrative qualities. We revel in a "melodrama" which is far removed from the classic union of spoken words and musical accompaniment, as practised in ancient Greece. Even "burlesque" (generally pronounced "burly-cue") no longer suggests actual parody or dramatic caricature, but rather the stabilization of the feminine leg, and a machine-gun fire of obvious double entendre.

Of all these characteristic institutions of the American theatre, minstrelsy alone has done credit to its name. It is a long way, perhaps, from the "minstrel" of the Middle Ages to the burnt-cork circle, centring in the pompous Interlocutor, and flanked by Bones and Tambo. Yet both the music and the quips produced by the traditional minstrel show have something in common with the extemporaneous efforts of their colourful ancestors.

> *"Gaily the troubadour touched his guitar,*
> *As he was journeying home from the war."*

The old song sums up the spirit of minstrelsy for all time in those much-quoted lines. The minstrel has always been a fighter as well as

I

an entertainer, first in the service of an individual master and later in the service of the public at large. Originally, he was literally a "minister" or servant, and it was probably the old law of human nature, that "no man is a hero to his own valet," that turned the ministering menial into a jaunty and indispensable jester.

As early as the Fourteenth Century, minstrelsy was a recognized profession in all the civilized countries of Europe. Its members were known variously as troubadours, jongleurs (or jugglers), bards, and glee men, in addition to the generic term "minstrel," and their spirit and habits were shared to some extent by the Minnesingers of Germany and even the more stodgy, formula-worshipping Meistersingers.

In those days, a minstrel had to develop his technique with a sword as well as a lute. His dance steps were likely to carry him literally among the lancers, with the smiles of court ladies for favours. The serenader of those days doubled in steel armour as well as brass, and his make-up was quite as likely to be a visored helmet as a mask of fashion or comedy. A "doleful ballad to his mistress' left eyebrow" might alternate at a moment's notice with a vengeful back-stroke at his enemy's left ear.

Minstrelsy in the Fourteenth Century, as in the Nineteenth, was no child's play, but a hardy man's game, full of danger and adventure. The gallant vocalist in doublet and hose, with a rapier on his left hip and a lute slung under the right shoulder, equally ready for a fight or a frolic, typified a combination of romance and daredeviltry which produced its modern descendants in the pioneering blackbirds of the minstrel road shows, equally gallant in their brave display of finery, and struggling against enemies and adversities quite as definite as those of the Middle Ages.

The old-time minstrel was both poet and press agent, and this dual capacity has also been preserved to some extent by tradition. He was maintained in comparative luxury by his noble patron, for the

INTRODUCTORY

express purpose of singing that patron's praises, as well as joining in his practical defense when the occasion arose.

Cyrano de Bergerac, who, with complete sang-froid, could compose a ballad while neatly puncturing the person of his adversary, is the prototype of the fighting poet, and there were many like him before and after.

François Villon damned the King and sang his praises in the same breath. The spirit of his song and the keenness of his blade won him the heart of a Princess. How could she help loving such a man?

King David was as handy with a harp as with a sling shot, and his music soothed the savage breast of Saul as effectively as his little pebble silenced the braggadocio of the giant Goliath.

The minstrel of Charlemagne rode into the fray juggling a huge battle-ax and singing the original Chanson de Roland.

Blondin, a gifted harpist, searched for his musical master, Richard of the Lion Heart, all over southern Europe, and finally discovered him in an Austrian dungeon, to the speedy restoration of a royal and loyal harmony.

The Scottish border had its famous minstrels, as Wales had its bards, and the harps of Ireland sounded not only "through Tara's Halls," but in so many other places that serious efforts were once made to limit by law the number of their professional and amateur exponents.

It is the demon of self-expression that has goaded on these minstrels, old and new, with perhaps the need of a meal-ticket adding its still, small voice in the background. This eternal combination of the temperamental and the practical has always urged men, and will always urge them, to travel through the world singing their songs, loving their ladies, and fighting their battles. There is little of logic, reason, or calculation in their lives. They are occupied with mirth, melody, poetry, and their public knows it.

Stranger, give us a song! If it be a jolly one, we shall laugh with you! If it be a sad one, we shall cry with you! If it be a song of wine, we shall drink with you, and if it be a ballad of a fair and false one, we shall sympathize with you. But if you sing it out of tune or time, we shall damn you to uttermost perdition!

Times and styles may change, but nature persists in reproducing the thoughts, the aspirations, and the accomplishments of mankind. So, as the circus clown shouts his familiar "Here we are again!" the Interlocutor of minstrelsy echoes the blander suggestion, "Gentlemen, be seated!" each reminding an endless audience of a showmanship built upon universal instincts, and still essentially the same.

The ebullient spirit of the ancient minstrel is still with us, and his modern representative has fought his battles and conquered his enemies just as surely as did his romantic ancestors. But these enemies were not feudal barons and their retainers. Rather were they the subtler but none the less definite ogres of circumstance, prejudice, financial and physical handicaps.

The "show business" is well acquainted with those courageous and optimistic troupes that travelled westward with no more substantial backing than a promise to pay if the box-office permitted, storming the frontier fortresses on a tenuous shoe string, with no weapons beyond a slender supply of "stock paper." Even the manager of such an outfit could make himself believe the gilded talk that has always been the vocabulary of the troubadour. The urge of self-expression was upon them all. The ignis fatuus of success danced before their eyes, and in too many cases it eluded their grasp.

It is reported that, in a single season, that of 1873–1874, eighteen out of thirty-nine minstrel companies went broke on the road, and

4

their members, sans wardrobe or other paraphernalia, wearily counted the railroad ties on their pedestrian way home.

An advance agent, waiting in New York for a troupe that was working its way down the Hudson one cold December, finally wired the manager, asking when he expected to arrive. The answer came back, collect, "On the next cake of ice."

There is another traditional story in the show business, dating back to the 1869 outfit of "Sharpley's Ironclads," concerning the German musician who, finding himself the only one not paid off, delivered the ultimatum, "I don't vash up till I get me some money!"—a remark which has been quoted a thousand times since.

Those were the days when the careful housewife would call to her neighbour, "Better get your clothes offen the line! Show folks in town!" The trouper's integrity was doubted even when his ability was appreciated.

It is a far cry from the primitive period of the "Big Four" (headed by Dan Emmett himself of "Dixie" fame) to the "Forty, Count 'em! Forty!" of the closing years of the past century. Many a long-

drawn "whoop" and lusty "holler" rent the air between the somnolent, whistle-tooting days of the '40's and the raucous, trombone-blaring era of the '90's. In that time the minstrel business developed from a four-man organization, working in a limited territory, to a series of great companies, well trained and gorgeously costumed, touring the country from coast to coast.

The climax of American minstrelsy lies well within the memory of the present generation. Less than fifty years ago this unique form of native art was at its height. The acorn planted by Dan Emmett and his companions had produced a mighty oak, rough though its bark may have been.

In the twenties, the minstrel show became chiefly an amateur pursuit, although the radio revived interest in its technique to such an extent that the minstrels of the microphone actually reappeared on the professional stage with marked success.

These pages, however, are set down chiefly in the spirit of reminiscence, and for the reader's own amusement; and for the present and future generations.

This "Parade of the American Minstrels" is by no means attended with ease and luxury. It may lead us into out-of-the-way places, full of discomfort and hardship. Occasionally, we may get stuck in the mud or held up for the price of a lodging.

But it will be an interesting adventure, none the less, with more than its share of romance and an optimistic coating of mirth and melody. "All aboard!" then, and let the human comedy begin!

II. THE DEVELOPMENT OF BLACK-FACE

IT HAS been argued that the first part ever played on the stage in "black-face" was Shakespeare's "sooty devil" Othello, in 1610. But as Othello was a Moor, and therefore of Arabian features, his character can hardly be considered in the Negro tradition.

A Boston advertisement, dated December 30, 1799, and thus barely catching the Eighteenth Century, states that in a performance of "Orinoko, or the Royal Slave," a Mr. Grawpner sang Negro songs in character make-up. The mysterious Grawpner, then, should be credited with being the first minstrel, in the American sense.

THE FIRST BURNT-CORKERS

Other early stage singers, however, seem to have blackened their faces for no particular reason, unless it was to disguise their identity. One of them was known as "Pot Pie" Herbert and his songs evidently had a practical use in helping to sell his pies. Incidentally, that great actor, Edwin Forest, is said to have given a serious and lifelike characterization in black-face when he played Cuff in a piece called "Tailor in Distress." But Thomas D. Rice, known affectionately in the profession as "Daddy" Rice, seems to deserve the credit of being the first to make a national or "race illustration" of the Negro character. He had heard an old darky in Cincinnati sing an authentic Negro ditty, with a shuffling accompaniment of the feet:

"Weel about and turn about and do jis' so,
Eb'ry time I weel about I jump Jim Crow."

7

T. D. RICE
THE ORIGINAL "JIM CROW"

This was the origin of the famous Jim Crow song, and perhaps of the title itself, commonly applied to the Negro race, and once used in the South for the car space allotted to the coloured people.

Rice worked out a song with appropriate business, from the hint given him by the shuffling old darky, and he gave his new act its first try-out in Pittsburgh. His final inspiration came from the grotesque appearance of an actual negro who hung around the theatre, and Rice finally persuaded him to lend his entire outfit for the occasion. Since the lender of the costume had no other, he was forced to wait in shivering deshabille, out in the alley, while the act went on.

The success of the song was so great that Rice had to respond to insistent encores. Finally, the forgotten Negro crept in through the stage door, and the song came to an abrupt end with his audible whisper from the wings, "Ah wants mah clo'es."

Here is the Jim Crow song as Daddy Rice sang it:

JIM CROW

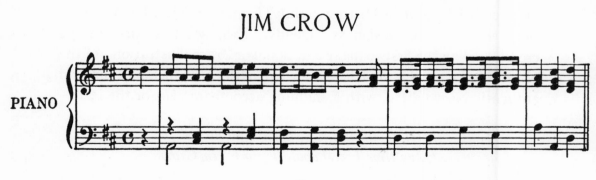

PIANO

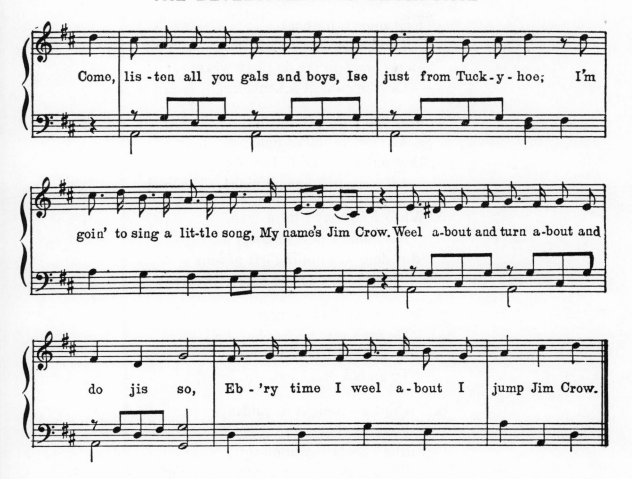

2. I went down to de river,
    I didn't mean to stay;
But dere I see so many gals,
    I couldn't get away. [*Chorus*]

3. And arter I been dere awhile,
    I t'ought I push my boat;
But I tumbled in de river,
    An' I find myself afloat. [*Chorus*]

4. I git upon a flatboat,
    I cotch de Uncle Sam;
  Den I went to see de place where
    Dey killed de Packenham.   [*Chorus*]

5. And den I go to Orleans,
    An' feel so full of fight;
  Dey put me in de Calaboose,
    An' keep me dere all night.   [*Chorus*]

6. When I got out I hit a man,
    His name I now forgot;
  But dere was not'ing left of him
    'Cept a little grease spot.   [*Chorus*]

7. Anoder day I hit a man,
    De man was mighty fat;
  I hit so hard I knocked him in
    To an old cockt hat.   [*Chorus*]

8. I whipt my weight in wildcats,
    I eat an alligator;
  I drunk de Mississippy up!
    Oh, I'm de very creature.   [*Chorus*]

9. I sit upon a hornet's nest,
    I dance upon my head;
  I tie a wiper round my neck
    An' den I go to bed.   [*Chorus*]

10. I kneel to de buzzard,
    An' I bow to the crow;
  An eb'ry time I weel about,
    I jump jis' so.   [*Chorus*]

FRANK BROWER

THE
ORIGINAL
BIG
FOUR
OF
MINSTRELSY

DICK PELHAM

According to these ancient pictures, the "Virginia Minstrels" might have sold patent medicines or cough drops with as much success as they gained behind the foot-lights with banjo, fiddle, bones, and tambourine. Their portraits present a neat exposition of the decline and fall of whiskers.

DAN EMMETT

UNTOUCHED
BY THE
DISGUISING
INFLUENCE
OF
BURNT CORK

BILLY WHITLOCK

DICK PELHAM   DAN EMMETT   BILLY WHITLOCK   FRANK BROWER

THE VIRGINIA MINSTRELS ("BIG FOUR")

AS THEY LOOKED TO AN ARTIST OF THEIR DAY

THE DEVELOPMENT OF BLACK–FACE

By the way, the first appearance of Joseph Jefferson on any stage was in black-face, as a partner of Daddy Rice, at the Bowery Theatre, Washington, D. C., in 1832. Jefferson, a tiny boy at the time, was carried on by Rice in a valise, emerging as a miniature "Jim Crow" and joining Rice in the song and dance.

Other Negro songs followed immediately after the success of Rice's experiment. *Zip Coon* (also known as *Turkey in the Straw*) became popular, and there were also *Clar de Kitchen, Lucy Long, Such a Gettin' Up Stairs, Gumbo Chaff, Sittin' on a Rail,* etc. But while the list of black-face performers grew rapidly, it was not until 1843 that anything like a real minstrel troupe existed.

This was the year of the organization of the immortal "Big Four," Dan Emmett, Frank Brower, Dick Pelham, and Billy Whitlock. Gaze upon their faces with reverence, for they were the real parents of American minstrelsy.

They met in a New York boarding house and worked out the idea of a four-man show. Whitlock claims to have been its originator, so why not give him the credit?

They called themselves the Virginia Minstrels and gave a benefit performance for Dick Pelham, which was followed by a real opening at the Bowery Amphitheatre, February 6, 1843. Their success was immediate and permanent. After delighting American audiences for three months, the Virginians sailed for England and monopolized the attention of London for another six weeks. The black-face minstrel had undoubtedly arrived.

Frank Dumont has claimed that performers in black-face appeared on a Philadelphia stage prior to 1843, but the "Big Four" seems to have been the first actual troupe to give a regular series of shows and to use the name of "minstrels."

The second troupe to be formed was known as the Kentucky Minstrels, and this group consisted of five men. After them came the Ring and Parker minstrels, followed by the "Congo Melodists," who later changed their name to Buckley's New Orleans Serenaders. They first appeared at the Tremont Theatre in Boston, but soon came to New York. Among other achievements they are credited with the first burlesque of grand opera, still a popular sport.

The next great name to appear in the line of minstrelsy was that of Edwin P. Christy, who appeared in Albany as early as 1844, although the organization known as the Christy Minstrels came somewhat later. At first there were four men, but in time two more were added, named Dickinson and Backus. Their New York debut was made at Palma's Opera House.

The Christy troupe went to England in the '50's and became so popular that their name was eventually applied generically to all Negro impersonators. The Christys also enjoyed the honour of having their name on one of the widely circulated "songsters" or pocket song books of the day.

Another company to win the hearts of London was that of the "Ethiopian Serenaders," consisting of F. Germon, G. Harrington, M. Stanwood, G. Pelham, and W. White. Their success was so great that they had to give morning as well as afternoon and evening shows, thus starting the "three-a-day" practice. They also appeared before Queen Victoria at Arundel Castle, by special command, and each member of the troupe was presented with a ring bearing the royal crest.

In a Philadelphia company known as the Virginia Serenaders there first appears the name of Cool White, later a very prominent minstrel. "White's Serenaders," headed by Cool and his brother, came to life in 1846, and this troupe included Master Juba, a famous coloured dancer. It is not certain whether he derived his name from the Negro "Juba Dance" or vice versa.

Then there were the "Harmoniums," organized in Boston, and the "Sable Harmonizers," whose roster included six names, Plumer, Archer, J. Farrell, W. Rorke, Nelson Kneass, and Murphy.

THE DEVELOPMENT OF BLACK-FACE

Within the next ten years, minstrel companies sprang up all over the country, and the American public first saw such giants of burnt cork as Dan and Jerry Bryant, Mestayer, Luke West, Kunkle, Sandford, Eph Horn, George Christy, and George Wood.

Campbell's Minstrels used the adjective "original," which soon became general, and in 1847 this troupe trod the boards at Barnum's American Museum. P. T. Barnum himself was capable of presenting a song and dance, and there is a record of his blacking up in place of an incapacitated minstrel and presenting *Such a Gettin' Up Stairs* and other favourites.

WHAT'S IN A NAME?

The impresarios of minstrelsy seem to have racked their brains for distinctive and descriptive names for their organizations. The "Sable Brothers" sounded logical enough, as did the optimistic "Nightingale Serenaders." But there were also "Ordway's Æolians" and the "Washington Utopians." Most of these companies also dignified themselves with the title of "opera troupe," and in some cases the word "empire" was inserted somewhere, to add to an already implied magnificence.

This was only the beginning. Duprez and Benedict called their aggregation the "New Gigantic Minstrels," and M. B. Leavitt invented the word "Gigantean." Primrose and West headed the "Mammoth Minstrels," and the same term was used by Barlow and Wilson. Richards and Pringle were content with a modest "Famous Georgia Minstrels," but Carncross insisted that his outfit was the "Star Troupe of the World."

Hi Henry advertised the "Superb Operatic Minstrels," while Barlow Brothers used both "Mammoth" and "Magnificent" in their posters. McNish, Johnson, and Slavin emphasized the word "Refined," which may have become necessary by that time. Primrose and West eventually compromised on BIG, but Colonel Jack Haverly

15

went into prehistoric biology again to unearth the soul-satisfying term "Mastodon." It was the big bass drum of this troupe that first carried the inscription, "Forty, Count 'Em! Forty!"

The Big Four had increased tenfold, and the circle of twoscore singers became a tradition for the full-sized minstrel show.

On the way to this climax there had been many experiments, with a full share of incongruities and absurdities. But minstrelsy survived them all.

The first "yodeller" among the minstrels was Tom Christian, who made his debut in Chicago in 1847. His falsetto tones thrilled the audiences of that city for seven years, and the Tyrolean "broken reed" eventually became a regular minstrel feature. It has now been relegated to the college campus and canoedling parties.

There was a black-face Dutchman as far back as 1858 in the person of Dave Wambold, of the minstrel team of Birch, Wambold and Backus. He is said to have possessed a really beautiful voice, which makes the anachronism of his Afro-Teutonic achievement all the more difficult to explain.

The great Billy Emerson, in 1868, showed an even stranger disregard of the fitness of things, when he did *The Old Clothes Man* in Hebrew dialect, without removing the burnt cork.

Jerry Cohan, on the other hand (father of the great and only George), introduced Irish brogue, Irish songs, and Irish jokes into the black circle. Some of his specialties were *The Dublin Dancing Master, The Dancing Professor*, and *Paddy Miles, the Irish Boy*. The elder Cohan was in minstrelsy as early as 1867, and became a famous end man and comedian long before he went into vaudeville as the head of the "Four Cohans."

(When actors speak of anachronisms, however, they usually find their climax in Corse Peyton's putting on a song and dance to finish an act of "Camille.")

Ordway's Minstrels, credited with originating the street parade about 1850, were also the first to put on a show in white-face, a precedent which has always been distrusted by true followers of minstrelsy. The white wigs, elaborate costumes, and gorgeous draperies were also looked upon with misgivings, some claiming that such a troupe looked more like a female burlesque company than a minstrel show.

It is worth noting, however, that many a later black-face artist eventually removed the familiar make-up and proved equally successful without the dusky disguise. Outstanding examples are Frank Tinney, Eddie Cantor (who originated the impersonation of the sophisticated "city chap," as represented by Octavus Roy Cohen's Florian Slappey), and finally Al Jolson, by way of the movies.

MINSTRELSY AS A STEPPING STONE

But American minstrelsy remains essentially a black-face proposition, and this book intends to view it exclusively from the darker side. In passing, it may be worth while to mention a few more celebrities of the stage who took their turn, at some time, in the semicircle of the traditional minstrel show. Joseph Jefferson, Edwin Forest, and P. T. Barnum have already been mentioned, although the first named belongs in the realm of "legitimate black-face" rather than in minstrelsy. Edwin Booth did a turn in black-face before he was known as a tragedian, and Patrick S. Gilmore, the great bandmaster, started as a minstrel.

David Belasco was never an actual minstrel, but it is an unquestioned fact that he played "Uncle Tom" at Shiel's Opera House, San Francisco, in 1873.

Denman Thompson of "The Old Homestead" was a successful end man before he became a dramatic star. Neil Burgess had his own minstrel show before he created Aunt Abigail in the "County Fair." Similarly, Joseph Murphy preceded his Irish plays, "Kerry Gow," "The Shaugran," etc., with an apprenticeship in minstrelsy.

J. K. "Fritz" Emmett, famous as a Dutch comedian, also started under the blanket of burnt cork, as did Barney Williams, originally known as "Dandy Jim from Caroline," and later a specialist in Irish melody.

Fred Stone first teamed with Dave Montgomery in Haverly's Minstrels. That was in 1895 in New Orleans. Nat Goodwin also was with Haverly as early as 1876. Joseph Cawthorne and Raymond Hitchcock were both originally minstrel men, and the latter picked up his old habits again when he went in as a pinch-hitter for "Honey Boy" Evans in the most elaborate of the modern troupes.

Chauncey Olcott was a favourite with the Carncross Minstrels, Primrose and West, and other companies, before he went in exclusively for Irish balladry; and Andrew Mack, most recently of "Abie's Irish Rose," and formerly a vaudeville star, dedicated his early stage career to black-face. Otis Skinner's first part on the stage was in black-face, in a piece called "Marked for Life."

Weber and Fields did a burnt-cork act before they discovered the advantages of German dialect. Carroll Johnson was known as the "Beau Brummel" of minstrelsy before he starred in "The Gossoon" and "The Irish Statesman," and later returned to his first love, playing at Dumont's in Philadelphia and with Lew Dockstader in New York.

George Fuller Golden, monologuist, and Billy Clifford, famous for his "chappie" impersonations, once teamed up in black-face. John Gorman, Harry Kernell, and many other names might be mentioned.

Willie Collier and De Wolf Hopper reversed the rule and took their turn at minstrelsy in a Lambs' show long after they had made their reputations with undisguised physiognomies.[1]

The minstrel show has been a training school as well as a recognized art form.

---

[1] Mr. Collier provided the information that his theatrical career actually began in minstrelsy also, but his role was that of selling song books for Haverly's Coloured Minstrels, at Niblo's Garden, New York. Later he became call-boy at Daly's Theatre and did his first real acting in Haverly's Juvenile Pinafore Company.

WILLIE AND BUSTER COLLIER *as Black Friars*

WEBER AND FIELDS *as Boy Prodigies*

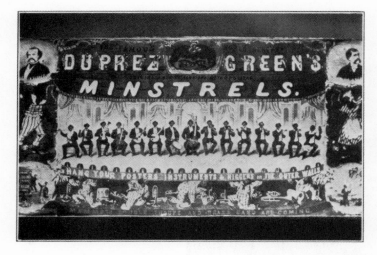

The complete minstrel circle, with comedians in the foreground, as shown in an old poster of the highly successful Duprez and Green troupe. ←

The Primrose and West Minstrels all ready to knock 'em dead at the local opry house. The two stars of the show are sitting at the (reader's) left end of the front row. →

Refined bally-hoo for a road show. The Minstrel Parade, flanked by its staunchest admirers, the small boys of the town, with the theatre itself in the background. ←

III. THE FIRST PART

IT IS hard to say just how soon the Minstrel Show crystallized into its accepted form (of which a practical outline will be found later in this volume). But it is certain that the first part of the programme, with the intermediate "olio," became a set tradition quite early. The second part remained a free fantasy, consisting of individual specialties, sketches, and often elaborate parodies of current plays, similar in many respects to the revues of later date. But the "First Part" had a definite technique, to which all minstrel men were unswervingly loyal, and which has been consistently observed throughout its history.

Essentially this part represents a running dialogue between the middle man, or "Interlocutor" (accented on the third syllable), and the two end men, known generally as "Bones" and "Tambo" because of the instruments which they played. This dialogue was interrupted at regular intervals by set songs, ponderously and portentously announced by the Interlocutor, with the whole company frequently joining in the chorus. In fact, the whole machinery of jokes and pompous persiflage existed chiefly for the sake of introducing these set numbers, just as a musical comedy has its dialogue built around a definite vocal programme. The songs were by no means all humorous, and in general it was a rule that the worst jokes should precede the best and most serious lyric efforts. At the end of the first part, there was a "walk-around" in which the entire troupe joined. The "olio" (played "in one") would then occupy the interval while the stage was set for the second part of the show. (The term "olio" has also been loosely applied to the entire first part.)

"GENTLEMEN, BE SEATED!"

THE PARADE

The actual parade of the old-time minstrels was the outgrowth of circus habits. It was soon realized that such advance publicity had a practical value, and long before the troupes grew to the size of "Forty, Count 'Em! Forty!" a parade from the railroad station to the local hotel was an established ritual.

The shrill pipe of a small boy, "Hey, fellers! Minstrels comin'!" was a better advertisement than a three-sheet poster. A group of youngsters was usually at the "depot" to see the 11:40 come in with its precious cargo. Later, most of the town girls managed to be somewhere along Main Street to see the parade go by, with much giggling and nudging of each other and an occasional exchange of bold glances with the gallant paraders.

The Silver Cornet Band always headed the parade, and the minstrels themselves marched four abreast if the company were sufficiently large, otherwise by twos, like the animals entering the Ark. Each man wore a long-tailed Newmarket coat of startling pattern, with

lapels of red silk, and on each head was perched a shiny "plug" hat. In front of the band marched the drum major, wearing a short red coat liberally encrusted with gold braid, and crowned by a towering shako of imitation bearskin. He juggled his brass-knobbed baton continuously, throwing it in the air and catching it in the manner of his ancestor of the Chanson de Roland.

The town boys lengthen their stride to keep up with the parade as it marches through Main Street, their faces sparkling with excitement, for to every small

22

boy the minstrel is a hero. At the Mansion House the parade comes to a halt. The band lines up at the door for a valedictory gallop or quickstep, and then follows the troupe in to dinner. The crowd of boys and girls, with a sprinkling of adults, disperses gradually, and the afternoon is spent in finding ways and means of attending the evening performance. (Usually the most effective method was the straightforward, "Gimme a quarter, Pa, to see the minstrels?" But times have changed!)

We are now at the Opera House, and it is nearly 8:15. The band has been tuning up in the basement. The minstrels have completed the process of blacking up, to the usual accompaniment of jokes and personalities. Out in the auditorium the audience is waiting expectantly.

The call-boy back stage makes his rounds with an "All up for the first part!" The band takes its place on a raised platform in the rear of the stage, while the minstrels stand in front of their allotted chairs in the semicircle.

The stage manager takes a quick look around to make sure that every man is in his place, rings a bell for the flyman, and up goes the curtain. There is a burst of applause from the audience. As it subsides, the man in the exact centre of the circle raises his voice in sonorous tones:

"Gentlemen, be seated!"

THE INTERLOCUTOR

The man who delivers this dignified pronunciamento, usually followed by "We will now commence the performance with the overture," is the one "straight performer" of the minstrel show. Tradition has given him the fittingly ponderous name of "Mr. Interlocutor," and he is the accepted master of ceremonies.

There is no suggestion of comedy in the full-dress suit and expansive shirt front of his costume. Sometimes he plays in white-face, contrasting with the black clowns on both sides of him, and his hair is usually his own, not the conventional kinky wig fitting closely to the head, or the elaborate comedy coiffure of Bones or Tambo.

The speaking voice of the Interlocutor must be resonant and suggestive of untold magnificence. Occasionally, he may render a ballad, and thus reveal that he is by nature a basso. But mostly his is a speaking part.

He is the father of all the foils in vaudeville, those well-dressed, gentlemanly fellows of unimpeachable manners, who speak such painfully correct English and are such easy prey for the low buffoonery of their companions. It seems absurd that so obviously intelligent a person could be so consistently outwitted in verbal exchanges, but it is one of the laws of human drama that this should be so.

The crowd likes nothing better than to see a half-wit get the better of a pompous intellectual. It restores confidence, as it were. And so the Interlocutor is the eternal buffer for the jocosities of his end men, the necessary "feeder" to their running stream of ribald clowning.

This give-and-take between the centre and ends of the semicircle has in it the necessary element of contrast, which brings the minstrel show almost to the level of actual drama. It is assumed that the Interlocutor will always get the worst of the exchanges. Yet he must never lose his dignity. He must continue patiently to correct the atrocious grammar and the impossible mispronunciations of the ignorant but immensely entertaining oafs, and he must be consistent in his apparent misapprehension of the most obvious jokes, his utter inability to answer the simplest of conundrums.

Whenever an end man scores a point, he is joined in boisterous laughter by his balancing colleague at the opposite end, and often by the entire troupe. This ancient device for creating immediate merriment seems also to have been borrowed from the circus, for there too it is the tradition that the clown shall always get the better of the ringmaster and laugh loud and long over his discomfiture.

It may be argued that the custom goes even further back in history, for it has been pointed out (by no less an authority than Brander Matthews) that in Sixteenth Century Paris a quack doctor was always accompanied by a jack-pudding, who propounded questions which the doctor answered in learned terms, whereupon the jack-pudding would proffer his own ribald explanations and thus raise a laugh from the crowd. Catch questions were known in Elizabethan England as "selling a bargain," and Shakespeare made frequent use of such comedy, often allowing his clowns to run on and off as they pleased. The dialogue of the  two Dromios in "The Comedy of Errors" is similar in substance to the traditional gagging of minstrelsy's end men.

Every type of farce must have its "stalking horse," the "fall guy" of modern slang, and this is the role of the minstrel Interlocutor. He is an impossibly correct individual, and his introductions of set numbers are couched in the most grandiloquent and florid language. No minstrel show could get along without him.

THE END MEN

If the Interlocutor is the keystone of the minstrel arch, the end men are the flying buttresses. (Or, to make a typical minstrel pun, he is the butt, etc.)

The Interlocutor's "Good-evening, Mr. Bones" is enough to

bring the whole audience to the edges of their seats, for they know that this simple greeting will inevitably lead to some side-splitting response from the rat-tat-tat comedian.

He derives his name from the rhythmic noise producer that he manipulates. A "set of bones" was originally an actual pair of bones,

MR. BONES

used in the manner of castanets. The cannibals of Africa probably originated the idea when they wanted a little music after having feasted thoroughly upon their enemies.

The rattling of bones is represented by the xylophone in Saint-Saëns's "Danse Macabre," and Shakespeare, in "A Midsummer Night's Dream," gives Nick Bottom the line, "I have a reasonable good ear in music, let us have the tongs and the bones."

It was in 1841 that the bones were introduced into minstrelsy, and Frank Brower, of the original "Big Four," was the introducer. He used the actual ribs of a horse, sawed to a length of twelve inches, and they provided a splendid rhythmic "kick." Many a boy of the past century tried to imitate Brower's invention, saving the bones from the family roast beef, drying and scraping them carefully, and then going to infinite pains to produce new patterns of rhythm with their clicking cooperation.

Later, the real bones of the minstrel show were replaced by sticks of ebony or some other hard material, and the clever end man would toss them in the air and catch them between his fingers, much as his legitimate descendant, the jazz drummer, now juggles his sticks and other paraphernalia of noise. There were both art and science in playing the bones of early minstrelsy.

THE FIRST PART

And what a ready wit Mr. Bones possessed, to be sure! How infinitely superior his homely phraseology to the studied correctness of Mr. Interlocutor! When the latter asked his conventional, "Well, Mr. Bones, how do you feel this evening?" the reply might be, "I feel just like a stovepipe." You quivered with the anticipation of mirth, as poor, blind Mr. Interlocutor walked right into the trap with his obedient, "You feel like a stovepipe? How is that, Mr. Bones?" Then came the explosion, with the end man's delicious answer, "A little sooty!" A cosmic jest in its day, but defying analysis! Of such was the kingdom of minstrelsy.

Mr. Bones, on the right end, is balanced by Mr. Tambo on the left. Sometimes they make a special entrance, with comic business, and sometimes there are two of them on each end. But the principle is the same.

Mr. Tambo gets his name from the tambourine, even more common than the bones as a noise maker. Sometimes the whole minstrel troupe would carry tambourines to punctuate the climaxes and sustain the chords. But the left end man was recognized as the virtuoso of the instrument.

It is hardly necessary to describe the tambourine in detail. Carmen and the Salvation Army have sufficiently popularized it. The name is derived from "tambour," meaning a shallow drum, and "tambourine" is its diminutive. France, Italy, and Spain encouraged its use long before it entered the circle of American minstrelsy.

The tambourine permits a rhythmic tapping of its single drum head, a whirling of its metal discs, and a general shaking of its completely loose and irresponsible mechanism. It is also a temptation to jugglery, and Mr. Tambo is a past master of that art. Up in the air, behind his back, under his chair, goes his tambourine, sometimes several tambourines at once, with knuckles, elbows, head, and feet paying rhythmic tribute to the endlessly moving sheepskin. Biff! Bang! Rattle! Whirr! With the bones adding their spirited click-clack, the two end men almost succeed in drowning out the band in the rear.

The final "walk-around" rises to a frenzied pandemonium of rhythmic sound. Bones and Tambo, leaning at an angle of forty-five degrees, and holding their noise makers high in air, sustain the climax as long as body and soul can stand the strain. A final triumphant chord from the band, and the curtain drops on the First Part.

MR. TAMBO

THE BANJO

Far more characteristic of American minstrelsy than either bones or tambourine, however, is the banjo, the legitimate musical possession of the Negro himself.

According to an old poem, originally published in *Harper's Magazine*, the banjo goes back to the time of Noah's Ark, and its origin was as follows:

THE ORIGIN OF THE BANJO

Go 'way, fiddle, folks is tired of hearin' you a-squawkin',
Keep silence for your betters, don't you hear de banjo talkin'?
'Bout de 'possum's tail she's gwine to lectur',—ladies, listen,
About de har dat isn't dar, an' why de har am missin'!

"Dere's gwine to be a overflow," said Noah, lookin' solemn,
For Noah tuk de *Herald*, an' he read de ribber column.
An' so he sot his hands to work a-clarin' timber patches,
An' vowed he's gwine to build a boat to beat de steamer *Natchez*.

THE FIRST PART

Ole Noah kep' a-nailin', an' a-chip-
    pin' an' a-sawin';
An' all de wicked neighbours kep'
    a-laffin' an' a-pshawin';
But Noah didn't mind 'em, knowin'
    what was gwine to happen,
An' fo'tty days, an' fo'tty nights,
    de rain she kep' a-drappin'.

The poem relates how the Ark
was finally completed, and the animals of all creation loaded in, how
the animals didn't care for their
strange surroundings, and that the
lions and tigers in particular made night and day hideous with their
roaring and caterwauling. The poem then proceeds:

Now Ham, the only jigger what was runnin' on de packet,
Got lonesome in de barber shop an' couldn't stan' de racket;
An' so, for to amuse hisself, he tuk some wood an' bent it,
An' soon he had a banjo made, de fust dat was invented.

Now de 'possum had as fine a tail as dis dat I'm a-singin',
De har was long an' thick an' strong, jest fit for banjo stringin'.
Dat jigger shaved 'em off as short as wash-day dinner graces,
An' sorted of 'em by de size, from little E's to basses.

He strung her, tuned her, struck a jig, 'twas "Nebber mind de Wed-
    der";
She sound like fo'tty-leven bands a-playin' all togedder;
Some went to dancin', some to pattin', Noah called de figures,
An' Ham, he sot an' knocked de tune, de happiest of jiggers.

29

Now since dat time, it's mighty strange, dere's not de slightest showin'
Of any har at all upon de 'possum's tail a-growin';
An' cur'us too, dat nigger's ways, his people nebber los' 'em,
For where you find de nigger, dere's de banjo an' de 'possum.

This is a pleasant fancy, but ethnological research proves that Africa actually possessed an instrument known as the "banjar," made of a large gourd, with a neck of wood attached, and fitted with four strings. It is quite possible that this primitive banjo came to America in the earliest days of Negro slavery.

The invention of the banjo as we know it, however, is generally credited to Joe Sweeney, a famous member of the early Virginia Minstrels. He took a cheese box, fitted it with a neck, attached five strings, and there you are.

Whether we bless or curse Sweeney for his invention, the banjo became the most popular instrument for accompanying Negro songs, and was an indispensable member of the original jazz bands. Today it is a major instrument in folk and country music.

The greatest banjo player of them all was E. M. Hall, whose wonderful feats are still remembered in stageland. (He was killed in the Iroquois Theatre fire in Chicago.) Banjo playing called not only for musical skill and dexterity, but for juggling ability as well. There are still performers who can juggle a banjo while playing a tune, and the same trick has long been used by country fiddlers.

The banjo largely gave way to the ukulele in the twenties, although its shape and general materials were adapted to the easier Hawaiian instrument, as well as to the mandolin. There was a time when every school and college was represented by a banjo club. The old group pictures are with us yet!

THE MINSTREL CIRCLE IN FULL SWING

NELSE SEYMOUR

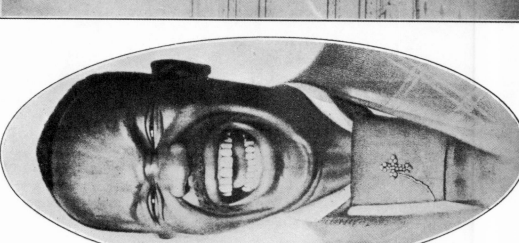

BILLY KERSANDS

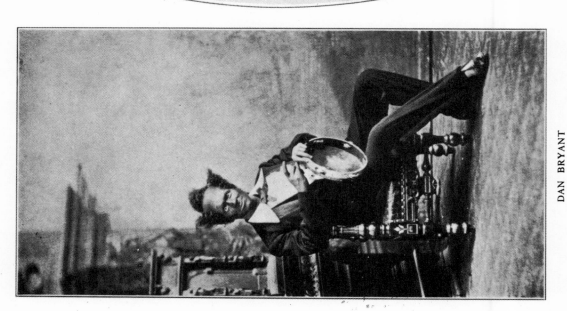

DAN BRYANT

The Bright and Dark Sides of Early Trouping

IV. SONGS THE MINSTRELS TAUGHT US

THIS would seem to be the right moment to put down some of the songs that stood out in the minstrel shows of the past. They were of all kinds, comic and serious, sentimental and ribald, naïve and sophisticated. Only a few specimens can be given here, but they are genuine.

Billy Emerson's *Big Sun Flower* necessarily stands first. It is one of the most famous of all minstrel songs, and reference is made to it several times in this book. Emmett's *Old Dan Tucker* is even better known to the general public, and it is said that there was an actual character of that name. The song appears in most of the old minstrel collections, along with *Root, Hog, or Die*, which eventually became a phrase of political significance.

Wake Nicodemus is a more serious type of song, with something of the atmosphere of a spiritual. In a contrastingly comic vein is *Dandy Jim of Caroline*, which also became in time a traditional phrase in the American language.

Josiphus Orange Blossom contains a rather heavy-handed humour, with direct reference to Civil War days and a curious echo, in the final stanza, of the English music-hall favourite, *Not for Joe*.

One of the less known but distinctly beautiful of the Foster songs is *Hard Times Come Again No More*. On the other hand, *I Hope I Don't Intrude* is again distinctly of the English school.

Stop dat Knockin' at My Door was one of the Christy favourites, with chances for plenty of action and clowning. Finally we have a typical Negro song, *Going to the Silver Wedding*.

33

THE BIG SUN FLOWER

There is a charm I can't ex-plain, A - bout a girl I've seen, My heart beats fast when she goes past, In a

dark dress trim'd in green. Her eyes are bright as

eve - ning stars, So lov - ing and so shy, And the

folks all stop and look a - round When ev - er she goes

CHORUS

by. And I feel just as hap - py as a big sun flow'r, That

35

nods and bends in the breez - es, And my heart is as light, as the

wind that blows, The leaves from off the tree - zees.

DANCE

D.C. Sym.

36

SONGS THE MINSTRELS TAUGHT US

As days past on and we became,
    Like friends of olden times,
I thought the question I would pop,
    And ask her to be mine,
But the answer I received next day,
    How could she treat me so?
Instead of being mine for life
    She simply answered "No." [*Chorus*]

I went next day dressed in my best,
    This young girl for to see,
To ask her if she would explain
    Why she had shaken me,
She said she really felt quite sad
    To cause me such distress,
And when I said "Won't you be mine?"
    Of course she answered "Yes." [*Chorus*]

OLD DAN TUCKER

Ole Dan Tuc - ker's come to town, So get out de way!

get out de way! get out de way,

Ole Dan Tuc - ker! you're too late to come to sup - per

2. Tucker is a nice old man,
   He use to ride our darby ram;
   He sent him whizzen down de hill,
   If he hadn't got up he'd lay dar still. [*Chorus*]

3. Here's my razor in good order
   Magnum bonum, jis hab bought 'er;
   Sheep shell oats, Tucker shell de corn,
   I'll shabe you soon as de water gets warm. [*Chorus*]

4. Ole Dan Tucker an' I got drunk,
   He fell in the fire an' kick up a chunk,
   De charcoal got inside he shoe.
   Lor' bless you honey how de ashes flew. [*Chorus*]

5. Down de road foremost de stump,
   Massa make me work de pump;
   I pump so hard I broke de sucker,
   Dar was work for ole Dan Tucker. [*Chorus*]

6. I went to town to buy some goods
   I lost myself in a piece of woods,
   De night was dark, I had to suffer
   It froze de heel ob ole Dan Tucker. [*Chorus*]

7. Tucker was a hardened sinner,
   He nebber said his grace at dinner;
   De ole sow squeal, de pigs did squall,
   He hole hog wid de tail and all. [*Chorus*]

ROOT, HOG, OR DIE

I'm right from old Vir-gin-ny wid my pock-et full ob news, I'm

worth twen-ty shil-lings right square in my shoes, It does-n't

make a dif of bit-ter-ance to nei-der you nor I,

Big pig or lit-tle pig, Root, hog, or die.

SOPRANO
ALTO

TENOR
BASS

CHORUS

I'm chief cook and bot-tle-wash-er, cap-tain ob de wait-ers; I

stand up-on my head, When I peel the Ap-ple dum-plins.

42

SONGS THE MINSTRELS TAUGHT US

I'se de happiest darkee on de top ob de earth,
I get fat as possum in de time ob de dearth,
Like a pig in a tater patch, dar let me lie,
Way down in old Virginny, where it's Root, hog, or die.   [*Chorus*]

De Boston dandies, dey look so very grand,
Old clothes hand me down, gloves upon de hand,
High heel boots, moustaches round de eye,
A perfect sick family ob Root, hog, or die.   [*Chorus*]

De Boston gals dey do beat them all.
Dey wear high heel shoes for to make demself's tall,
If dey don't hab dem, den Lor' how dey'll cry,
De boys hab got to get dem or else Root, hog, or die.   [*Chorus*]

De Shanghie coats dey're getting all de go,
Where de boys get dem I really don't know,
But dey're bound to get dem if dey don't hang too high,
Or else dey make de Tailors run Root, hog, or die.   [*Chorus*]

43

WAKE NICODEMUS

up!"was his charge, "at the first break of day, Wake me up for the great Ju-bi-lee!"

SOPRANO
ALTO

CHORUS

The "Good Time Coming" is al-most here! It was long,long,long on the

TENOR
BASS

way! Now run and toll E-li-jah to hur-ry up Pomp, And

meet us at the gum tree down in the swamp, To wake Nic-o-de-mus to-day.

45

"GENTLEMEN, BE SEATED!"

He was known as a prophet—at least was as wise—
    For he told of the battles to come;
And we trembled with dread when he rolled up his eyes,
    And we heeded the shake of his thumb.
Tho' he clothed us with fear, yet the garments he wore
    Were in patches at elbow and knee;
And he still wears the suit that he used to of yore,
    As he sleeps in the old hollow tree.   [Chorus]

Nicodemus was never the sport of the lash,
    Tho' the bullet has oft crossed his path;
There were none of his masters so brave or so rash,
    As to face such a man in his wrath.
Yet his great heart with kindness was filled to the brim—
    He obeyed, who was born to command:
But he longed for the morning which then was so dim—
    For the morning which now is at hand.   [Chorus]

'Twas a long, weary night—we were almost in fear
    That the future was more than he knew;
'Twas a long, weary night—but the morning is near,
    And the words of our prophet are true.
There are signs in the sky that the darkness is gone
    There are tokens in endless array,
While the storm which had seemingly banished the dawn,
    Only hastens the advent of day.   [Chorus]

DANDY JIM OF CAROLINE

Allegretto

PIANO

I've oft - en heard it said ob late, Dat Souf Ca' - li - na was de state, Whar hand - some dan-dy's bound to shine, Like

Dan - dy Jim of Car - o - line, For my ole mas - sa
tole me so, I'm do best look-ing dandy in de coun-try oh, I
look in de glass, an' I found it so, Just as mas - sa
rall.
tell me, oh.

2. I drest myself from top to toe,
   And down to Dinah I did go,
   Wid pantaloons strapped down behind,
   Like Dandy Jim of Caroline. (*Refrain*)

3. De bulldog cleared me out ob de yard,
   I thought I'd better leabe my card,
   I tied it fast to a piece ob twine,
   Signed "Dandy Jim of Caroline." (*Refrain*)

4. She got my card, an' wrote me a letter,
   An ebery word she spelt de better,
   For ebery word an ebery line,
   Was Dandy Jim of Caroline. (*Refrain*)

5. Oh, beauty is but skin deep,
   But wid Miss Dinah none compete;
   She changed her name from lubly Dine,
   To Mrs. Dandy Jim of Caroline. (*Refrain*)

6. An ebery little man she had,
   Was de berry image ob de dad,
   Der heels stick out three feet behind,
   Like Dandy Jim of Caroline. (*Refrain*)

7. I took dem all to church one day,
   An' hab dem christened without delay,
   De preacher christened eight or nine,
   Young Dandy Jims of Caroline. (*Refrain*)

8. An' when de preacher took his text,
   He seemed to be berry much perplexed,
   For nothing cum across his mind,
   But Dandy Jims of Caroline. (*Refrain*)

JOSIPHUS ORANGE BLOSSOM

My name it is Jo-si-phus Or-ange Blossom, I'm the gay - est Col - or'd Gem-man in the land, With the pret - ty girls I al - ways plays the Pos - sum, I'm a

Red Hot Hun-ky Do-ry Con-tra-band. When first I fell in love with Jane Me-

lis-ser, I tried my best to win from her a smile, I

caught her round the waist and tried to kiss her, Says

she go'way I does-n't like your style. Guess not,

Red hot, I'm the gay - est Col - or'd Gem-man in the land, Oh! my

name it is Jo - si - phus Or-ange Blossom, I'm a Red Hot Hun-ky Do - ry Con-tra-

band.

D.C.

SONGS THE MINSTRELS TAUGHT US

I thought my Jane Melisser was a beauty,
  So I popped the question to her Sunday night.
Says she, "I think you are the one to suit me,
  Your company always gives me delight."
I told her that I thought she was perfection,
  Upon her charming face my eyes could feast,
And if she had no serious objection,
  Next Sunday night we'd patronize the priest.

Wa'n't she sweet? Hard to beat?
  She was the blithest creature in the land,
And I know she loves Josiphus Orange Blossom,
  I'm a Red Hot Hunky Dory Contraband.

One evening sweet thoughts were o'er me creeping,
  I thought upon my sweetheart I would call,
As in her window slyly I was peeping,
  I saw something that did my heart appall,
Her teeth and one eye laid upon the table,
  Her pretty curls were hanging on a peg,
I laughed aloud as hard as I was able,
  To see her taking off a wooden leg.

Oh, no! Not for Joe!
  I can't take Melisser for a wife,
So out of town I soon got up and dusted,
  I never was so sold in all my life.

HARD TIMES COME AGAIN NO MORE

Let us pause in life's pleas-ures and count its man-y tears; While we all sup sor-row with the poor; There's a song that will lin-ger for-ev-er in our ears; Oh!

Hard times, come a - gain no more.

CHORUS
'Tis the song, the sigh of the wea - ry; Hard Times, Hard Times,

come a - gain no more, Man - y days you have lin - gered a -

round my cab - in door; Oh! Hard Times, come a - gain no more.

"GENTLEMEN, BE SEATED!"

While we seek mirth and beauty and music light and gay
    There are frail forms fainting at the door;
Tho' their voices are silent, their pleading looks will say, oh! [*Chorus*]

There's a pale, drooping maiden who toils her life away,
    With a worn heart whose better days are o'er;
Tho' her voice would be merry, 'tis sighing all the day, oh! [*Chorus*]

'Tis a sigh that is wafted across the troubled wave,
    'Tis a wail that is heard upon the shore,
'Tis a dirge that is murmured around the lowly grave, oh! [*Chorus*]

I HOPE I DON'T INTRUDE

must not think me rude,— For love it is the bur-den of my song; With

joy I'm al-most cra - zy, And if per-chance, I sing or dance, You must not think me

rude, And if per-chance I sing or dance, I hope I don't in-trude.

CHORUS

Oh! dear, don't you wish that you were me?

I

feel just as hap-py as a big bum-ble bee. I was

walk-ing by her door When I heard the mu-sic sweet; My heart with joy filled

o-ver, And I could not keep my feet, So keep the mu-sic ring-ing, As it

makes me feel so good, And if I make a lit-tle break, You must not think me

SONGS THE MINSTRELS TAUGHT US

rude. And if I make one lit-tle break, I hope I don't in-trude.

DANCE

At a fancy ball the other night, myself and little Daisy,
  We kept it up till broad daylight, we felt so awful good,
And Daisy looked so fair and bright, she set the men all crazy,
  And when they'd ask her for to dance, she'd say, "I wish I could."
  Then I would say, in careless way, "I hope I don't intrude."
    [*Chorus*]

Blithe and happy be the summer day when I shall wed with Daisy,
  Then the merry birds will sing their lay, and wild flowers scent the
    wood,
Then the cares of life I cast away, my mind shall then be easy,
  And one and all, if you will call, we will not treat you rude,
  No, if you come to see our home, we'll say you don't intrude.
    [*Chorus*]

STOP DAT KNOCKING AT MY DOOR

I once did lub a col-ord Gal ____ Whose name was Su - zy Brown, She came from old Vir - gin - ny, She was de fair - est in de town, Her eyes so bright dey

shine   at night when   de moon am   gone___ a - way,   She

used   to call dis dar-key up ___   Just a - fore de broke of

day: wid a who dar? who dar?   who dar?   An' a

who   dar a-knock-ing at my   door?   Am dat   you Sam? Am

knocking. Stop that knocking. Oh you better stop that knocking at the door.

Let me in. Let me in. No I'll nev-er stop that knocking at the door.

CHORUS

1st TENOR
2nd TENOR

Stop that knock-ing, stop that knock-ing, stop that knock-ing, stop that

BARITONE
Melody
BASS

Stop that knock-ing, stop that knock-ing, stop that knock-ing, stop that

knock-ing, Oh! you bet-ter stop that knock-ing at my door. Stop that

knock-ing, No! I'll nev-er stop that knocking at your door. Let me in. Stop that

knock-ing, stop that knock-ing, stop that knock-ing, stop that knock-ing, Oh! you

knock-ing, stop that knock-ing, stop that knock-ing, stop that knock-ing, No! I'll

bet-ter stop that knock-ing at my door.

nev-er stop that knock-ing at your door.

8va

8va

64

SONGS THE MINSTRELS TAUGHT US

She was the prettiest yaller Gal that eber I did see,
She never would go walking wid any coloured man but me.
And when I took my Banjo down, and played three tunes or more,
All at once I heard, three pretty hard raps come bang again' my door.
Wid who dar? who dar? [*Chorus*]

Oh, de first one dat cum in de room was a dandy dressed to death,
He looked just like de showman, what dey used to call Mackbeth.
He said he was a Californi man, an' just arrived on shore,
I ax him whare fore he cum an' rap, so hard against my door.
Wid who dar? who dar? [*Chorus*]

GOING TO THE SILVER WEDDING

There's going to be a Sil-ver Wed-ding, We're all in-vit-ed down, And

there you'll have a chance to see The high-toned darks in town. There's

Jo - nas Clark, and Un - cle Storm Who wears a num - ber 'lev'n, Say

they'll be in with the high-toned darks, Down at the Sil-ver Wed-ding.

CHORUS

Pos - sum, sweet po - ta - toes, were sit - ting on the

SONGS THE MINSTRELS TAUGHT US

There's old Aunt Hannah and Uncle Pete, who're getting along in
    years,
Said that they are going down t'attend this grand affair.
At night when they were leaving home, how lightly they were tread-
    ing,
The children asked them, "Where you bound?" "We're gwine to de
    Silver Wedding." [*Chorus*]

If you're going to the Silver Wedding, be quick, it's nearly time;
Put on your clothes and let us go, 'fore the sports drink all the wine;
Frank Hart said that he would start, and be there prompt at seven,
To show the presents that he got, down at the Silver Wedding.
    [*Chorus*]

FOUND IN THE ARCHIVES OF MEMORY

Some of the oldest minstrel songs have literally disappeared
from sight, and are no longer to be found in printed form. A few
samples of such almost forgotten material are added here, as supplied
by the recollections of older heads than those of the author and the
editor.

One famous song that goes all the way back to slavery days is
The Gum Tree Canoe, which started like this:

> All day in the field of soft cotton I hoe,
> I think of my Judy, and sing as I go.
> I caught her a bird with a wing of true blue,
> And at night rowed around in my gum-tree canoe;
>
> *Chorus:*
> Roll away, roll away, waters so blue,
> Like a feather we'll float in my gum-tree canoe.

"GENTLEMEN, BE SEATED!"

Of *The Little Octoroon*, closely associated with the Civil War, only the second verse and chorus are remembered, as follows:

Then the brave old gunner took her in his arms.
Thinking of his own dear ones at home.
And through all the marches, and the rude alarms,
Safely brought the Little Octoroon.

Chorus:

Glory, glory, how the freedmen sang!
Glory, glory, how the old woods rang!
'Twas the loyal army sweeping to the sea,
Flinging out the banner of the free!

Can anyone to-day remember the rest of the song?

There are people all over the United States to-day who cherish the recollection of such homely ditties. Absurd as they may have been, there is about them an endearing quality, and the pity is only that they are so rapidly fading into oblivion.

Billy's Dream, however, the star number in the repertoire of Billy Arnold, can be supplied in its entire text, from the archives of memory:

BILLY'S DREAM

I had a fight with old Satan last night,
    As I lay half awake.
Old Satan he came to my bedside,
    An' me began to shake.
He shook me long, an' he shook me strong,
    He shook me clear out of bed;
Then grabbed me by the collar, an' looked me in the face,
An' what do you think he said?

70

SONGS THE MINSTRELS TAUGHT US

[The Minstrels: "What did he say, Uncle Billy?"]

Chorus:

There's gold in the mountains,
There's silver in the mines,
An' it all belongs to you, Uncle Bill,
If you only will be mine.

[Repeat by Minstrels.]

2.

He dragged me to the window, an' says, "Look there!"
The moon it shone quite bright,
An' the little hills an' the mountains grand
Shone clear unto my sight.
"Dear William," sez he, "these will all be yours,
If you'll be my gen'ral when you're dead";
I grabbed him by the collar, an' looked him in the face,
An' what do you think I said?

[The Minstrels: "What did you say, Uncle Billy?"]

Chorus:

Get ye gone, Mister Satan,
You've come here for to kill,
You may fool the white folks wid that trash,
But you can't fool poor black Bill.

[Repeat]

3.

I was feelin' kinda chilly, so I crep' back,
An' crawled me into bed;
An' all night long in my dreams I saw,
My dear Lord His head.

"GENTLEMEN, BE SEATED!"

Ole Satan done vanished through the floor,
 An' a light on me it shed;
I threw the covers right off my face,
 An' the Lord to me He said;

[*The Minstrels: "What did he say, Uncle Billy?"*]

Chorus:
 "Well done, faithful servant,
  You may sit at my right hand,
  An' play on the golden harp all day,
  Although but a poor coloured man."
[*Repeat*]

V. THE REINCARNATION OF JOKES

LIKE that fabled bird with asbestos feathers, the Phœnix, that rose from dead ashes to flap its wings in derision of the flames that had raged around it, so do jokes lie dormant and apparently lifeless for years, only to spring into life again at a wave of the magic wand of some professional jester. The form may be changed a bit, but the germ of the joke is the same.

So it is with stories which have for their foundation certain dramatic or comic situations. They live, and live again, recast in the minds of story-tellers, borrowed consciously or unconsciously from their original sources, and refurbished until they take on the semblance of originality and newness.

"Men may come, and men may go, but jokes go on forever." And so do stories for that matter.

Plagiarism came in about the time Cadmus invented letters, and has flourished ever since.

Mr. Dooley says, "It's my story because I told it last."

Kipling makes his confession in the much-quoted lines:

> *"When 'Omer smote 'is bloomin' lyre,*
> *He'd 'eard men sing by land an' sea;*
> *An' what he thought 'e might require,*
> *'E went an' took—the same as me!"*

Shakespeare's writings are full of puns, jokes, and plays on words which, with slight modifications, still pass current as witty material. Minstrelsy has made use of the same jokes over and over again, many of them dating back to ancient literature.

On the other hand, the old minstrel shows have provided plots and situations, not to speak of "gags" and "hokum" for much of the modern stage material. The pun has been called "the lowest form of wit," a mere reflex action in the association of sounds. Quite logically, therefore, the pun is the staple fare of minstreldom. But the popularity of punning goes much further back in history than this.

The minstrel men probably got their terrible punning habit from the English writers of pantomime and extravaganza. This was not exactly a case of reincarnation, but of transplanting a weed among the flowers of rhetoric.

Malapropisms have always flourished in the minstrel show, particularly when imitating the speech of the Negro, who loves big words and lots of them, and can mispronounce them and get their meanings tangled with grace, facility, and generally comic effect.

Conundrums have also furnished a large stock in trade for the humorists of the minstrel show. (See the discussion of the end men and Interlocutor, pp. 23-28.) The more absurd the answer supplied by the end man, the better for chuckles. The propounding of conundrums is one of the oldest methods of joke making, older than history, old as mythology; and still new ones are propounded every day, many of which are old ones dressed in the modern vernacular.

Here are a number of old minstrel "wheezes" which have been used in many forms. Several of them occur in Hughey Dougherty's "Oratorical Stump Speaker," a source book for much comic material.

Q. When was the theatrical business first spoken of in the Bible?
A. When Eve appeared for Adam's benefit.

Eddie Foy, in "Piff, Paff, Pouf," gave the Adam and Eve joke a new twist which has been often repeated since:

Q. Why was Eve made?
A. For Adam's Express Company.

THE REINCARNATION OF JOKES

Here is another of international flavour:

Q. What language does an Arabian child speak before it cuts its teeth?
A. Gum Arabic.

The same wheeze appears in "Erminie," when Ravvy is telling what a distinguished linguist his friend Caddy is. The Princess asks, "You say your friend speaks Arabic?" And Ravvy answers, "Certainly, gum Arabic."

Animal jokes and puns have always been popular. This one is from Dougherty's book:

Q. Why do hens lay in the daytime?
A. Because at night they become roosters.

The next is almost too simple to be true, but it still lives:

Q. What has a cat got that nothing else has?
A. Kittens.

This nautical experiment is rather far-fetched:

Q. Where do ship captains keep their poultry?
A. In the hatchway.

And here is one for which Seth Thomas, the clockmaker, fired a working man back in 1818:

Q. What is always behind time?
A. The back of the clock.

(Seth said he made Grandfather's clocks, but didn't like Grandfather's jokes.)

In a joke book printed nearly sixty years ago, under the heading "Gags," occurs the following cross-fire talk between middle man and end man, the substance of which is used as a mental test question in our schools to-day:

MIDDLE: Did you see me coming home with a gun over my shoulder?
END: Yes; where did you go?

75

"GENTLEMEN, BE SEATED!"

MIDDLE: I was out shooting. There was no game!

END: You didn't have your cards with you, did you?

MIDDLE: As I said before, I found no game. I was returning home rather disappointed, when I saw on a fence, not a dozen yards from me, five crows.

END: What colour were the crows?

MIDDLE: Black, of course. Now, tell me—I shot one, how many were left?

END: Any fool knows that. Why, there was four left.

MIDDLE: No, sir, I knew you couldn't tell me. Now try again.

END: You say there wasn't four left? Now, let's see; five cows sitting on a fence.

MIDDLE: Five crows, not cows.

END: Yes, crows. You come along with a deadly weapon concealed about your person. You sneak up to these unsuspecting crows, and you aim at the biggest crow. He's sittin' there chattering with glee, not dreaming that death lurks in such close proximity to his person. You blaze away; the fat crow drops. He's dead—he's defunct! He's obliterated! He's gone to that place from where no feller gets back! Now you want to know how many is left? Four! You can't get out of it. Four left.

MIDDLE: You're wrong! When I fired my gun, and killed one crow, the rest flew away; consequently, there was none left. Ha, ha! Ha!

(It will be noted that contrary to tradition, the joke is here on the end man.)

Here is a Negro yarn that dates back about one hundred years and had a rebirth in New York shortly after the completion of the subway as far as Harlem.

A traveller in the South inquired of a Negro the distance to a certain place, and received this reply:

"Dat 'pends on circumstances, massa. Ef you gwine afoot, it'll take you 'bout a day; if you gwine de stage or de honeybus, you make it in half a day; but if you git in one of dese smoke wagons, you almost dar now."

The New York Negro answers an inquiry about the distance to Harlem and how to get there in a similar manner:

"If you gwine by de cars what runs on top de ground, it takes you 'bout two hours. If you git in one of dem upstairs cars, it takes you 'bout half an hour; but if you goes down dat hole in de ground and gits a car, you is dar now."

76

THE REINCARNATION OF JOKES

A very old gag, whose descendants are more numerous than humorous, is the following:

"Ed, who was that girl I saw you walking with the other day?"
"Why, that was my fiancée."
"Yes? What's her name?"
"Helen French."
"What is it in English?"

(The commonest variant of this joke is the line about going to "Helen Hunt" for it.)

Another antediluvian is the one about a sign reading, "Families supplied here." A man, seeing the sign, goes into the store, lays down two dollars and says, "Give me a wife and two children."

This gag has not only been told on the stage many times but has been put into lyric form as a verse for a comic song.

The one about the man who hates women, who decides to get away from women, to go and live alone on a desert island and there bring up his children also to hate women has been doing duty for lo, these many, many years.

When one hears a joke that bears the earmarks of antiquity, it is generally fastened upon Joe Miller, author of a famous book of witticisms. But the writer of a little pamphlet entitled "Fun in Black," published in 1874, goes far back before the days of the redoubtable Miller. According to this writer, a certain Hierocles, in the Sixth Century, originated and collected twenty-one jests, under the title of "The Pendant," and, "remarkable as it may seem, these humorous efforts have been retained, with variations, without becoming obsolete or threadbare."

This may have been true in 1874.

The same pamphlet tells a story about Harry Stanwood, the minstrel, which has been related many times since, with a different actor in the leading role each time.

Stanwood was an inveterate story-teller and jokesmith. While riding in a street car in Philadelphia with a companion, he was, as usual, pouring stories and jokes into his companion's ear. Just as he had finished what he considered a particularly clever one, the conductor of the car called out "Chestnut!" Stanwood jumped up and exclaimed: "Chestnut! That ain't no chestnut! I'll bet you ten dollars you never heard that one before in your life."

One of the jokes in "The Pendant" is the request not to go near the water until one has learned how to swim. It is possible that this admonition was the great-grandparent of the once popular ditty:

"Mother, may I go in to swim?"
"Yes, my darling daughter;
Hang your clothes on a hickory limb,
But don't go near the water."

Still good for years to come is the comparison of diamonds with chunks of ice. ("Cracked ice from Tiffany's" is the way it appeared in "Within the Law.") Eph Horn, a famous minstrel, pulled it in front of Tony Pastor's theatre many years ago. He noticed a piece of ice on the sidewalk. "Look at that," said Eph. "Pastor has lost one of the stones out of his diamond pin." The remark was widely quoted, for Pastor's diamonds outdid even those of Jim Brady.

One of the stand-bys of minstrelsy, of course, has been the familiar "Who was that lady I seen you with last night? That was no lady; that was my wife."[1]

There are plenty more of the same vintage still going the rounds.

Physical jokes and properties are just as likely to repeat themselves as merely verbal whimsies.

It seems to be a weakness of human nature to enjoy seeing someone run the risk of injury, and a comic stage fall has always been a sure laugh, particularly when accompanied by a whack on the bass drum. It is equalled as sure-fire material only by the application of the

---

[1]To-day, when they use this joke, they substitute "your wife" for "my wife."

slapstick, which incidentally provides the plot for most of the comic strips of the day.

The Romans enjoyed gladiatorial combats because someone was sure to get hurt. In a stage presentation, when a comic character falls and skids along on the back of his neck, the joy of the audience is complete and ineffable.

Catering to this eternal desire for a practical joke of purely physical significance came the device known as "the slippery day stairs."

The stairs were made after the manner of window shutters, with a bar running down them at the back, to which the stairs were fastened. When a lever attached to the bar was pulled, the stairs would close up, affording an ideal sliding place for the unsuspecting victims of the joker handling the lever.

To see an actor catapulting down these trick stairs always brought forth rapturous roars. "Slippery day stairs" were for years a standardized prop in minstrelsy. An old act, called "A Slippery Day," was frequently requisitioned to exploit this favourite laugh producer, and it was from this act that the stairs got their name.

When the "slippery day stairs" became a tale too often told in minstrelsy, it was reincarnated in several different fashions by producers of farce comedies, and even in semi-serious productions. In ship scenes the stairs leading to the bridge were often of the "slippery day" variety.

The idea was used by Charles E. Hoyt in a rather individual fashion, in his famous play, "A Temperance Town." The scene is the exterior of the village church, time, evening. The congregation is seen filing in to listen to a temperance sermon by the pastor. While the services are in progress, the town drunkard, horrible example of the curse of rum, enters, lugging a treadmill. The drunkard is tired and puts the treadmill down with one end resting on the steps of the church.

It does not look like a "plant," for the drunkard's actions do not indicate his intention to play a practical joke; he simply wishes to relieve himself of the treadmill until he is rested.

Soon after, the closing hymn is heard inside the church, the door opens, and as the worshippers step on the cleats of the treadmill, they begin to revolve, and the whole congregation, including the preacher, make hasty and undignified descents to the sidewalk. Curtain. "Man wants but little here below," particularly in the way of a joke.

THE REINCARNATION OF JOKES

Many people stop to wonder, and say to themselves: Who thinks up these silly jokes? Well, if you try to sit down and create a joke, it just won't happen. It's got to come—as Irving Berlin said in his song—"Doin' What Comes Natur'lly."

And this is the way one of these silly jokes occurred to me:

It was during jury duty in a New York courthouse while I was waiting, with others, to be called to serve in the jurors' box. Just sitting there, just waiting, with nothing to do, my restless mind was stirring up notions. It was playing out a dialogue sequence for a minstrel show. To wit:

(The End Man, Tambo, to the Interlocutor:)

TAMBO: Mister Interlocutor, what did the thief get who stole the judge's watch?

INTERLOCUTOR: I don't know, Mister Tambo, what did the thief get who stole the judge's watch?

TAMBO: "TIME, Mister Interlocutor, *TIME*."

* * * * *

Now, you are supposed to laugh at this . . . at least the perpetrator of the joke hopes so.

> "Laugh, and the world laughs with you;
> Weep, and you weep alone;
> For the sad old world must borrow its mirth,
> But has trouble enough of its own."
>
> Ella Wheeler Wilcox
> (1855-1919)
> "Solitude," Stanza 1

"GENTLEMEN, BE SEATED!"

WANTED: MORE LAUGHS

Love of laughter is the one characteristic that distinguishes man from the beasts.

Everyone appreciates laughter in all its forms, from a school girl's giggle to a teamster's guffaw. There is no finer, cleaner humour than that contained in the old-time minstrel shows. True, they date back to the first laugh, but a good joke, like a beautiful statue, never grows old. It can be enjoyed by generation after generation.

The good, hearty laugh that follows a wholesome joke is always well relished. It is truly a part of our daily diet, and without it we would wither and die, like flowers without sunshine.

And minstrelsy is the one constructive form of humourous entertainment that can be of cheer to alleviate the stress of realism.

VI. THE SECOND PART

HERE technique is thrown to the winds, and formulas of every kind are forgotten. If the first part of a minstrel show paralleled the exposition of themes in a symphonic movement, the second part represented the development or "free fantasia" of classic form.

The particular capabilities of any given troupe had much to do with the character assumed by the second part of their show. Individual specialties had a chance to shine in the "olio." Burlesque and parody ran riot, and often a complete drama, including some serious situations, was presented as an "afterpiece."

It has already been suggested that the second part of the typical minstrel show fathered the elaborate revues of modern times. We still have the individual specialties, the team acts, one playing "straight" and one comic, ending in a song and dance, the short sketches, and the elaborate burlesques of current drama. Weber and Fields were perhaps the first to introduce parodies into their musical shows, and their example has been widely followed.

The minstrel "afterpiece" was a typical product of its day, with original themes and situations, and the material of these afterpieces has proved a treasure-house for modern writers of musical comedy and farce, who have not hesitated to appropriate whatever they considered of value.

(Incidentally, it was interesting to see, in the former "Ramblers" of Clark and McCullough, a "good-bye" scene effectively worked up in the exact manner of the *"buona sera"* episode in Rossini's ancient "Barber of Seville." The continued reappearance of the actors, after they have said good-bye many times, gets just as many laughs as it ever did.)

83

"GENTLEMEN, BE SEATED!"

The great Harrigan and Hart shows all had the characteristics of "afterpieces" and were built out of what was essentially minstrel material.

Dancing specialties, of the buck and wing and clog variety, were nearly always included in the second part of the show. Stump speeches were also popular, giving special opportunities to the monologue artists of the company.

STUMP SPEAKERS

With actual orators and lecturers running rampant all over the country, a burlesque stump speech was not a difficult achievement. Local gags could be worked into such a speech *ad libitum*, to add to the sure laughs.

Two of the most famous stump speakers of minstrelsy were Hughey Dougherty and Billy Rice. Dougherty was a Philadelphia product, and although he did his share of road work, more than half of his career was spent at Frank Dumont's old minstrel palace, the Eleventh Street Opera House in Philadelphia. Reference has been made to Dougherty's book of stump speeches, jokes, and gags. It is full of broad humour, almost too broad at times even for present-day consumption.

Billy Rice used the earnest, strenuous method of putting over his speeches, somewhat in the manner of the late Sam Bernard, who always had to make at least one sputtering speech in every show. Rice's chief property was a cotton umbrella, which he would swing and bang effectively to emphasize his points. He worked for most of the big minstrel managers, Haverly, Emerson, Hooley, and others, and was also a partner in several companies. Of the whole Rice family, prominent and prolific in minstrelsy, Billy was the best stump speaker.

Musical acts fitted in well with the second part of the minstrel show, particularly the kind that displayed unusual versatility, with one performer exhibiting his skill on ten or twelve different instruments. This type of act is still popular in the vaudeville shows, and is closely related to the Swiss bell ringers, the marimba specialists, etc.

THE DARK TRIANGLE

Sex did not enter appreciably into the minstrel shows, beyond the inevitable double entendre of some of the jokes. But the afterpieces often had a plot of the triangle type, and the woman in the case was, of course, played by a man, and therefore frankly burlesqued.

As in the traditional college shows, the mere fact that a husky, deep-voiced male impersonates a female seems to have an irresistibly comic implication, and the more exaggerated the burlesque femininity, the more the audience likes it. The traditional climax of mirth has always come when the simpering "lady" suddenly displayed a pair of huge feet, emerging from dainty skirts, and preferably topped by unmistakably masculine trousers.

The ability to play a "wench" (the regular term for female impersonations) was a real asset in the minstrel business, and most of the great comedians included some such parts in their repertoire.

Dan Gardner, a comedian who starred as early as 1836, is credited with having played the first black-face "wench," and in the later afterpieces of the big minstrel shows, female characters of all kinds are common. A favourite seems to have been the termagant landlady, whose discomfiture the rest of the company always enjoyed with more than a professional enthusiasm.

A Christy playbill of 1857 shows an afterpiece called "The Toodles, with Curtain Lectures" (the relationship to Mrs. Caudle is obvious), and in the cast is the name of "G. Holland" who played the

part of "Mrs. Araminta Belinda Caudle Toodles." This is the same George Holland who was denied a Christian funeral service by a New York minister (God save the name!) but whose friends eventually found tolerance in the rector of the Church of the Transfiguration on Twenty-ninth Street. It was in connection with the Holland funeral that this house of worship was first called "the little church around the corner," a name that has stuck to it ever since.

M. S. Pike was another "wench player" of the '50's, and a prolific song writer as well. One of his best-known songs was *Home Again*, a very popular ballad in its day.

Wood's Minstrels, in 1865, featured Henry Wood, the head of the troupe, as Mrs. Puffy, in the afterpiece. Billy Birch, of the San Francisco Minstrels, was the "leading lady" in "The Female Brokers of Wall Street," in 1870. Charlie Backus, of the same troupe, was famous for his characterization of Mrs. Splutter in a farce called "Our Hash House", played in 1877 and written, it may be imagined, with a venomous pen.

William Henry Rice had the part of Fanny Crusty in "The Arrival of Patti," described as "a screaming farce." His reputation for wearing beautiful feminine costumes greatly antedated that of Julian Eltinge, and it is said that he actually set the styles in the towns he visited and made life miserable for the thrifty local husbands.

Lew Dockstader is still remembered for his playing of a burlesque "Camille," and the same company contained Willis P. Sweatnam, who starred as the Princess in "Our Minnie," a take-off on that reigning success at the Casino Theatre, "Erminie." (This was the same Willis

THE SECOND PART

P. Sweatnam who not so many years ago showed modern audiences how a Negro character part could be played, in his flawless portrayal of the coloured porter in "Excuse Me.")

Another female impersonator of the Eltinge type was "the only Leon," of Kelly and Leon's Minstrels, whose costumes were noted for their dainty attractiveness. He was an excellent ballet dancer and could give the impression of femininity even while running the gamut of the classic routine. Leon was billed as Galatea in the 1876 performance of "Galatea's Black Sculptor," and he appeared in a burlesque of Offenbach's opera, "The Grand Duchess," called "Dutch S."

The "great Ricardo" was prominently billed as a "high-class wench" with the San Francisco Minstrels and other companies. Of Eugene d'Anseli, known simply as "Eugene," it was said that he could easily deceive any audience not previously aware of his real sex. He played "fashionable ladies" abroad as well as in America, and Berlin theatregoers insisted that "Eugene" was actually a woman. But why argue about such matters?

Tony Hart, of the famous Harrigan and Hart team, has been described as the finest wench of his day, in either black-face or Irish make-up.

The pictures of old minstrel characters show many others who could represent a female convincingly, such as Burton Stanley, Stuart, and the Russell Brothers, who both played in black-face before vaudeville claimed them. One of Jimmy Russell's famous lines, in the part of a dignified lady talking to her servant girl, was "Maggie, take that cow out of the hammock!" Yes, they laughed at it then.

Perhaps the secret of success in the second part of the old minstrel show was its spontaneity. It shared with all folk music and folk literature the spirit of improvisation.

"GENTLEMEN, BE SEATED!"

Actually much of the material was put together on the spur of the moment and adapted to local needs and the news of the day. Old situations could be used over and over again. Ancient plots were undoubtedly resurrected, as they still are. But the atmosphere of the "afterpiece" remained extemporaneous, and it was its very freedom from restraint, its lack of all formality, that provided its greatest charm.

THE GREAT RICARDO

VII. A WORKING MODEL

FOR those who might like to know exactly how the lines of an old-fashioned minstrel show actually sounded, as well as those who may wish to try their hand at an amateur revival of this practical and still popular form of entertainment, a working model is here given, containing some of the traditional material of minstrelsy and easily adapted to whatever expansion may be necessary or desirable. This model gives details of the first part, and suggests possibilities for the "olio" with a complete "afterpiece" added independently.

Imagine, then, the semicircle of black-face actors, with each man seated in his chair, the end men in absurd and elaborate farce costumes, the middle man, or Interlocutor, immaculate in his evening clothes, the rest perhaps conventionally garbed. The overture has been played (any snappy march will do), and it may be that an opening chorus has been added of personal and local significance.

That famous tune of Spanish War days, *A Hot Time in the Old Town To-night*, makes splendid material for any kind of local parody. It is given here in its melody line, with the original words (the complete music being procurable from the publishers) to which is added the suggestion of a special text used with great success by the Radio Minstrels, both on the air and in the presence of an actual audience.

The opening chorus may be sung in unison or in harmony, but a lusty volume of sound is always desirable. Occasionally this musical number is announced by the Interlocutor, after his opening salutation.

"GENTLEMEN, BE SEATED!"

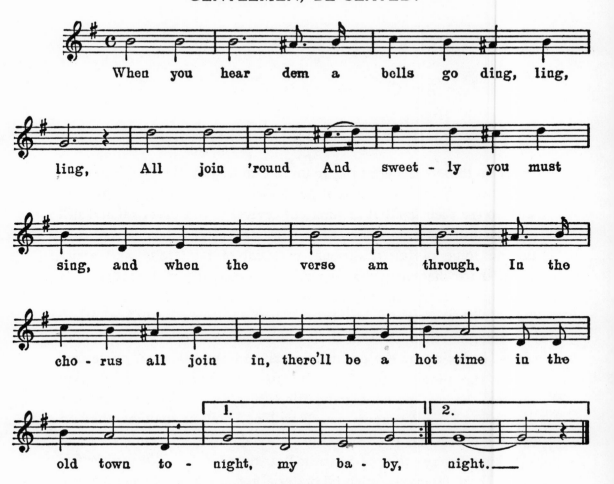

When you hear dem a bells go ding, ling, ling, All join 'round And sweet-ly you must sing, and when the verse am through. In the cho-rus all join in, there'll be a hot time in the old town to-night, my ba-by, night.

Bang! Bang! Bang! you will hear the tambos ring!
The old-time gang will show you they can sing;
And with a whang! whang! whang! and a zinga, zinga, zing!
There'll be a hot time in the old town to-night! And all those
Good old tunes will ring out loud and clear,
Dandy coons in their nifty acts appear;
And we all hope that you our Minstrel Show will cheer;
There'll be a hot time in the old town to-night!

A WORKING MODEL

We are now ready for the traditional dialogue and its interpolated numbers:

INTERLOCUTOR: Gentlemen, be seated. (Chord in G, accompanied by Tambourine.) Well, Mr. Bones, how are you feeling this evening?

BONES: Very well, Mr. Interlocutor, and how are you—how are all your folks?

INTERLOCUTOR: We're all well, excepting my brother. You see, a team of horses ran away with him, and he's been laid up ever since.

BONES: That's a very strange coincidence, same thing happened to my brother.

INTERLOCUTOR: You don't say.

BONES: The only difference is, it was my brother who ran away with the team of horses; he's been laid up ever since, but they'll let him out next month.

INTERLOCUTOR: My brother is convalescing, but we have to watch him very closely. You see, he's a somnambulist, and he's liable to have a relapse.

BONES: My goodness, a slambulnalisist, what's dat?

INTERLOCUTOR: Not a slambulnalisist, a somnambulist, one who walks in his *sleep*.

BONES: Oh, you mean a policeman. (*All laugh.*)

INTERLOCUTOR: I hear they've got a machine now that can tell when a man's lying.

BONES: Yessuh, I married one. (*All laugh.*)

TAMBO: Say, how can I drive a nail without hitting my fingers?

BONES: Hold the hammer in both hands, you darned fool. (*All laugh.*)

INTERLOCUTOR: Say, Mr. Bones, weren't you at some wedding yesterday?

BONES: Sure, I was to a wedding, and everybody had a good time too. The guests arrived in taxicabs and left in patrol wagons. The only one who got in without an invite was a Mexican Swede named Maginnis. He must have been a janitor because he said he came to clean up the place.

INTERLOCUTOR: Then what happened?

BONES: He forgot to bring his implements and so he used me for a mop.

INTERLOCUTOR: That was cruel of him.

BONES: Cruel indeed! Why, even my wife got so tender-hearted she couldn't bear to see me get hurt. So every time he knocked me down she just picked me up and brushed me off. After he had knocked me down about ten or fifteen times, I said to my wife, "Look here, the next time he knocks me down, you just let me lay." (*All laugh.*)

INTERLOCUTOR: Tambo, you were at that wedding. Did the bride get many presents?

TAMBO: Sure she did. Why, she received a hundred silver spoons.

INTERLOCUTOR: You don't say, a hundred silver spoons!

TAMBO: Sure, three were marked Sterling and ninety-seven were marked Pullman. (*Laughs.*)

INTERLOCUTOR: What strikes you so funny?

TAMBO: (*Laughs*) After the minister pronounced their doom, my brother asked him how much he owed, and the minister said, "Pay me whatever you think it's worth." (*Tambo laughs aloud above all others.*)

INTERLOCUTOR: Well, what are you laughing at now?

TAMBO: He's the first man I ever heard of who was willing to work for nothing.

INTERLOCUTOR: Our silver-voiced

tenor will now render that ever-popular ballad of blessed memory *When You and I Were Young, Maggie,* assisted by the quartette!

WHEN YOU AND I WERE YOUNG, MAGGIE

we used to, long a - go. The green grove is gone from the

hill, Mag-gie, Where first the dai - sies sprung; The

creak-ing old mill is still, Mag-gie, Since you and I were young.

CHORUS

And now we are a - ged and gray, Mag-gie, And the tri - als of life near - ly

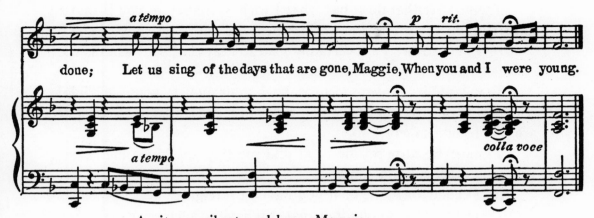

done; Let us sing of the days that are gone, Maggie, When you and I were young.

A city so silent and lone, Maggie,
Where the young and the gay and the best,
In polish'd white mansions of stone, Maggie,
Have each found a place of rest,
Is built where the birds used to play, Maggie,
And join in the songs that were sung:
For we sang as gay as they, Maggie,
When you and I were young. [*Chorus*]

They say I am feeble with age, Maggie,
My steps are less sprightly than then,
My face is a well-written page, Maggie,
But time alone was the pen.
They say we are aged and gray, Maggie,
As spray by the white breakers flung;
But to me you're as fair as you were, Maggie,
When you and I were young. [*Chorus*]

INTERLOCUTOR: Now, Tambo, tell me, how are *you* feeling this evening?

TAMBO: In the language of the Poets, Mr. Interlocutor, I exalts! I exalts!

INTERLOCUTOR: I'm afraid, Mr. Tambo, that I don't quite understand you.

"GENTLEMEN, BE SEATED!"

TAMBO: Neither do I, but what I wish to convey to you is that I am sittin' on the top of the world—mentally and physically—Wow!

INTERLOCUTOR: I am certainly glad to hear that. But what is the cause of this feeling of exuberance?

TAMBO: Oh, Mr. Interlocutor, hush your mouth, you is terrible!

INTERLOCUTOR: Well, Tambo, so as to make it easy for you, why are you feeling so gay?

TAMBO: Because my best gal told me that she loved me better than any other man in America.

INTERLOCUTOR: Ah, then you haven't foreign rights?

TAMBO: I never thought of that. I'll have to keep my eye on that ice man from Hoboken. (*All laugh.*)

INTERLOCUTOR: By the way, Mr. Tambo, are you interested in the Einstein theory?

TAMBO: No, sir; they always stick to my teeth.

INTERLOCUTOR: No, no. The Einstein theory is not a food. Why, Professor Einstein is the smartest man on earth.

TAMBO: So *he's* the other guy! I always knew there was two of us.

INTERLOCUTOR: Why, you fool, Professor Einstein wrote about the theory of Relativity.

TAMBO: Oh, he only *wrote* about them, but I've been *livin'* with my relatives for twenty years.

INTERLOCUTOR: No, no. You are all wrong. Why, his theory is the most difficult thing in the world to understand.

TAMBO: No, it ain't.

INTERLOCUTOR: Then what is?

TAMBO: The most difficult thing to understand is a conversation between a Chinaman and a Swede, in which the Chinaman is trying to explain to the poor Swede why it is he stutters.

INTERLOCUTOR: Our sweet singer of spiritual and secular ditties will now interpret *Ring Dat Golden Bell*, with the help of the chorus.

RING DAT GOLDEN BELL

One night I had a pleas-ant dream, Ring dat bell for glo-ry, I

sail'd me up de sil-ver stream, Ring dat gold-en bell. Bob

In-ger-soll was hard at work, Ring dat bell for glo-ry; De

an-gels told him not to shirk, Ring dat gold-en bell.

CHORUS
2nd time pp

Ring dat bell at de gold-en gate, Come you sin-ners, don't be late, Hur-ry on,

Bells

don't stop long, Ring-ing at de gold-en bell, Ding a ling a ling. bell.

A WORKING MODEL

I'd like to meet you all up there,
    Ring dat bell for glory,
And punch your tickets for de fare,
    Ring dat golden bell.
Old Jakey Sharp he won't be dar,
    Ring dat bell for glory,
Dey'll bounce him from de Broadway car,
    Ring dat golden bell. [*Chorus*]

I had another dream one night,
    Ring dat bell for glory,
Miss Langtry fought with all her might,
    Ring dat golden bell.
And Mary Walker jumped and danced,
    Ring dat bell for glory,
And tore her bran new Sunday pants,
    Ring dat golden bell. [*Chorus*]

Two countries tried to make a name,
    Ring dat bell for glory,
But neither had the pluck or game,
    Ring dat golden bell.
The Russian bears and British hams,
    Ring dat bell for glory,
Dey weakened like a pair of lambs,
    Ring dat golden bell. [*Chorus*]

Come all you sinners, watch your load,
    Ring dat bell for glory,
Don't race your horses on de road,
    Ring dat golden bell.

"GENTLEMEN, BE SEATED!"

You'll hab no Comstock in de sky,
    Ring dat bell for glory,
And you can gamble on the sly.
    Ring dat golden bell. [*Chorus*]

INTERLOCUTOR: Now, Tambo, you seem to be anxious to say something.

TAMBO: Yes, Mr. Interlocutor, I do feel the inclination of exercising my mouth.

BONES: Little fellow, you'se just like a frog.

TAMBO: What you mean, Big Boy, I'm like a frog?

BONES: Why, you all mouth, Boy, all mouth.

TAMBO: Hush, I was just going to ask the Interlocutor a question.

INTERLOCUTOR: Well, then, ask it, Tambo.

TAMBO: You ever go to the races, Mr. Interlocutor?

INTERLOCUTOR: Oh, yes, indeed. I'm very fond of horses.

TAMBO: Then do you know how to make a slow horse fast?

INTERLOCUTOR: Why, no, how do you make a slow horse fast?

TAMBO: Why, just don't feed him. (*All laugh.*) You know I went to a race last week; there were four horses in this race, and off they started. Snowball at the quarter and La Grippe at the half. Snowball, Pickles, and La Grippe came into the stretch neck and neck, and just as Snowball and La Grippe came to the finishing post—in flew Enza! (*All laugh.*)

INTERLOCUTOR: Did you ever back a horse, Mr. Bones?

BONES: Yes, sir. A friend of mine down at the track told me to bet on Bridge. He said it was a walkover. Another fellow told me to bet on Gold-digger. He said she'll get your dough. But I just took my own tip and played a horse named Hebrew. He won by a nose.

INTERLOCUTOR: Our own little Mr. Tambo will now entertain us with his original specialty.

A WORKING MODEL

(If Tambo does a clog dance, or plays the fiddle or banjo, the old *Arkansas Traveller* will be found a good tune.)

(If the Interlocutor wishes to sing a song, here or elsewhere, a bass solo of the following type is always effective. This chorus represents one of the stock numbers of the old-time bass organ-stoppers.)

con spirito

When the bell__ in the light-house rings ding dong,__ When it clangs__ with its warn-ing loud and long;__ Then a sail-or will think of his sweet-heart so true,__ And long__ for the day__ he'll come back__ to you,__ And his love__ will be told in the bell's brave song,__ When the

poco rit.

bell__ in the light-house rings ding dong. ding! dong! ding! dong! When the

Lento ben marcato

bell in the light-house rings ding dong, ding dong, ding dong!__

A WORKING MODEL

BONES (*Laughing*): Ha, ha, ha, ha!

INTERLOCUTOR: Here, here, what means this sudden burst of laughter?

BONES: I was just thinking of a tombstone.

INTERLOCUTOR: I don't see how you can laugh when you think of tombstones.

BONES: I was thinking of an epitaph on the tombstone of an automobile driver.

INTERLOCUTOR: What was the epitaph?

BONES:

> Here lies the body of William Jay,
> Who died maintaining his right of way.
> He was right, dead right, as he sped along,
> But he's just as dead as if he'd been wrong. (*All laugh.*)

TAMBO: I heard about one man that died and he met this Mr. Salt Peter.

INTERLOCUTOR: You mean Saint Peter, not Saltpeter.

TAMBO: Yeh, that's it. Saint Peter, standing at the gate.

INTERLOCUTOR: Yes, yes, and then?

TAMBO: Well, this Salt Peter, I mean Saint Peter, he was asking everybody where they come from, and some he would let in and some not.

INTERLOCUTOR: Well, that was natural. We can't all expect to enter the heavenly gates.

TAMBO: No, sir. That's the hell of it.

INTERLOCUTOR: Stop swearing and go on with your story.

TAMBO: Well, finally, this man came up to Salt Saint Peter, and he was from California.

INTERLOCUTOR: Ah, yes. California. Land of balmy breezes, of citrous fruits and fragrant flowers, where every prospect pleases, and every day is Springtime, where birds carol their lovely melodies all the year round, where the sun sheds its soft radiance by day and the stars smile upon exotic landscapes by night, where——

TAMBO: Yes, that's what I said. California. Well, when he told Saint Peter he was from California, Saint Peter he considered a minute and then he said, "Well, you can come in, but you won't like it." (*All laugh.*)

BONES: Say, Tambo, why do people always cry at weddings?

TAMBO: Because they've all been married before, and know what the poor fools are up against.

INTERLOCUTOR: Why is it that widows can get married so easily?

BONES: 'Cause dead men tell no tales.

TAMBO: Why is it they call the groom's attendant the best man?

BONES: Well, he's the best off, ain't he?

TAMBO: Does a man take a woman for better or for worse?

BONES: I don't know much about the woman, but I know the man will get the worst of it.

TAMBO: Why is it the woman takes the name of the man she marries?

BONES: Well, she takes everything else, so she might as well take that, too.

TAMBO: Do you think a wife should work for a husband?

BONES: I certainly do, until she gets him, and then she sure will work him.

INTERLOCUTOR: Mr. Tambo, what kind of a woman did you marry?

TAMBO: I married a regular umpire.

INTERLOCUTOR: Your wife is an umpire?

TAMBO: Yessuh, my wife is just like the regular Big League Baseball Umpire.

INTERLOCUTOR: Why is your wife like a baseball umpire?

TAMBO: Because she never thinks I'm *safe* when I'm *out*.

BONES: The trouble with you, Tambo, is that you allow yourself to be dictated to. Why, the other day I fell down a whole flight of stairs.

A WORKING MODEL

TAMBO: How did that happen?

BONES: Because, when I started to go down the stairs, my wife said, "Be careful you don't fall."

TAMBO: Yes?

BONES: Well, I'm the kind of man who never lets any woman dictate to him, so I fell down the whole flight of stairs.

TAMBO: Say, Mr. Interlocutor, I answered an ad in the paper to-day, and I sure run against a tough one.

INTERLOCUTOR: Well, what happened?

TAMBO: This man said to me, "Now, young man, what we want is a night watchman that'll watch, alert and ready, for the slightest noise or indication of burglars—somebody who can sleep with one eye open and both ears open and is not afraid to tackle anything."

INTERLOCUTOR: Well, I am positive you filled the position.

TAMBO: You're crazy. I sent my wife around. (*All laugh.*)

INTERLOCUTOR: Our mellifluous, harmonious, and glorious quartette will now oblige with that gem of melting beauty, *Aura Lee*.

AURA LEE

Male quartet.   *Arranged by Sigmund Spaeth*

A WORKING MODEL

On her cheek the rose was born,
   'Twas music when she spake;
In her eyes the rays of morn
   With sudden splendour break. [*Chorus*]

(*Cross-fire between Bones and Tambo.*)

BONES: Dat music makes me feel so happy!

TAMBO: Well, you ain't going to be happy no more. You're going to be a soldier and I'm going to train you. I'm a first-class soldier trainer, I is. I'm a regular lion trainer, I is.

BONES: You is a lion trainer?

TAMBO: That's what I said. I'se a hard-boiled lion trainer, I is.

BONES: You'se a lion son of a gun.

TAMBO: What's that you said—what's that you said?

BONES: I said I'd like to be trying that gun.

TAMBO: When I says you try that gun, you'll try it and not before. Remember, I'se de boss. Has you made up your mind to be a good soldier, boy?—Cause, if you hasn't, I'se going to start right in to make it up for you.

BONES: Of course I is, of course I is.

One of our defenders

TAMBO: Now, soldier, if you was to see the enemy coming, would you run or would you follow me?

BONES: I'd be doing both, because, if any enemy approaches, I'll be running right behind you.

TAMBO: Was your pappy a soldier?

BONES: Yessir, he was at the battle of Bull Run. He was one of the ones that ran. He had a horse pistol, my father did.

TAMBO: You mean a hospital?

BONES: No. A horse pistol. He raised it from a Colt.

TAMBO: Did he ever do anything brave?

BONES: Yes. At one time he saved a whole regiment from being killed.

TAMBO: How come?

BONES: He killed the cook.

TAMBO: I'm going to see how much of the army you know. Attention! Did you hear what I said? I said, Attention!

BONES: Ain't I attention?

TAMBO: You is attention from your knees up but from your knees down you're at parade rest.

BONES: What's the matter with my feet?

TAMBO: You done got them too close to the ground.

BONES: They're my feet, ain't they?

TAMBO: Of course they is your feet.

BONES: They're under me, ain't they?

TAMBO: Of course they is under you.

BONES: I'se on top of them, ain't I?

TAMBO: Of course you'se on top of them, but if all the men in the army had feets as big as them, they'd only be able to get two on the parade ground at once. I can see you got in the wrong branch of the service.

BONES: What do you mean the wrong branch? What am dis—a tree?

TAMBO: Yes, you might call it a tree, because you can bark around but they never let you leave. You ought to be in the aviation service.

BONES: What for?

TAMBO: Because you're no good on earth. Say, boy, was you ever around when there was any bullets flying?

BONES: I was, once, when a crazy man started shooting.

A WORKING MODEL

TAMBO: Did you run?

BONES: I wouldn't exactly call it running, but I done passed some folks that was running.

TAMBO: Then you didn't get hit in the fracas?

BONES: No, I had that well covered.

TAMBO: What did you have it covered with?

BONES: With my handkerchief.

TAMBO: Then you didn't get hit?

BONES: I didn't get hit, but I heard one of them bullets two times.

TAMBO: You heard one of them bullets two times?

BONES: Yessir. I heard a bullet when it passed me and I heard it again when I passed it.

TAMBO: Man, you is a coward. You know what we do with cowards in the army? We shoots them. We shoots them all at sunrise.

BONES: Then I'm sorry, mister, I just can't help you out, 'cause I never get up till the middle of the afternoon. (*All laugh*.)

INTERLOCUTOR: Our golden-voiced baritone will sing that touching ballad, *Darling Nelly Gray*.

DARLING NELLY GRAY

Con espressione

PIANO

There's a

low green val - ley on the old Ken-tuck-y shore, There I've

whiled man-y hap-py hours a - way, A - sit-ting and a-sing-ing by the

"GENTLEMEN, BE SEATED!"

When the moon had climbed the mountain, and the stars were shining
  too,
  Then I'd take my darling Nelly Gray,
And we'd float down the river in my little red canoe,
  While my banjo sweetly I would play.   [*Chorus*]

One night I went to see her, but "She's gone!" the neighbours say,
  The white man bound her with his chain;
They have taken her to Georgia for to wear her life away,
  As she toils in the cotton and the cane.   [*Chorus*]

My canoe is under water, and my banjo is unstrung,
  I'm tired of living any more,
My eyes shall look downward, and my song shall be unsung,
  While I stay on the old Kentucky shore.   [*Chorus*]

My eyes are getting blinded, and I cannot see my way;
  Hark! there's somebody knocking at the door—
Oh! I hear the angels calling, and I see my Nelly Gray,
  Farewell to the old Kentucky shore.

Final Chorus
Oh! my darling Nelly Gray, up in heaven there they say,
  That they'll never take you from me any more,
I'm a-coming—coming—coming, as the angels clear the way,
  Farewell to the old Kentucky shore.

  INTERLOCUTOR: Now, Tambo, didn't that song touch you?
  TAMBO: No, but the fellow that sang it did. He still owes me five.
  INTERLOCUTOR: Enough! Enough!
  TAMBO: He sure has got enough from me, I'll say he has.
  INTERLOCUTOR: I am astonished at you. Why, the idea of a man

of your mental calibre talking about such sordid matters, right after listening to such a beautiful song! Have you no sentiment left?

TAMBO: No, I haven't got a cent left.

INTERLOCUTOR: I didn't say cent, I said *sentiment—sentiment* —the tender thought that rules the world—the language of the flowers—the music of Mendelssohn—all that arouses sweet feelings. Why, man, can't you feel?

TAMBO: I feel he ain't never going to pay me my five back. (*All laugh.*)

INTERLOCUTOR: I'm afraid that music, the divine attribute of genius, does not appeal to you—music, the subtle harmonies of which have led men to battle for their country, to die without a thought of the future.

TAMBO: When they die, how are they going to pay me my money back?

INTERLOCUTOR: I'm not talking about money, but about music. Doesn't it soothe you? Music hath charms to soothe the savage breast, and you have no love for music! Bones, do *you* love music?

BONES: I should say I do. Why, whenever I hears music, my heart goes bumpity-bump.

INTERLOCUTOR: You're mistaken, your heart does nothing of the kind.

BONES: I guess I ought to know what my heart is doing.

INTERLOCUTOR: I tell you that you are mistaken. Your heart has nothing to do with your emotions. Your heart has no feeling, it is dumb.

BONES: My heart is bum?

INTERLOCUTOR: Not bum—dumb!

BONES: I got a bum heart?

INTERLOCUTOR: No, you haven't a bum heart. What I mean is that it isn't in your heart that your feeling exists.

BONES: It is.

INTERLOCUTOR: It isn't.

BONES: Say, whose heart is this, anyhow? (*All laugh*.)

INTERLOCUTOR: Tambo, I hear you were up before the judge the other day. What seemed to be the reason for your being summoned?

TAMBO: Well, I'll tell you, Mr. Interlocutor, I was summoned to appear befo' de judge fo' participatin' in rollin' out those African dominoes.

INTERLOCUTOR: Oh, I see, you were playing dice.

TAMBO: Yessir, that's it.

INTERLOCUTOR: Well, what did the judge say to you?

TAMBO: Why, he jest sed, "I'm going to fine you ten dollars," and I hurriedly put my hand in my pocket and I sed, "Judge, here's the ten dollars, I got it right here in mah pocket"; an' he looked at me and said, "All right, now—all right, now."

INTERLOCUTOR: All right, what did he say? "All right, now?"

TAMBO: He turned to me and sed, "All right, now, just look in your other pocket an' see if you got ten days." (*All laugh*.)

TAMBO: I got a poem I can recite.

INTERLOCUTOR: Well, go ahead and recite it.

> Mary had a little lamb.
> With her it used to frolic.
> It licked her cheek in play one day
> And died of painters' colic. (*All laugh*).

Bones bursting out:
> Mary had a little lamb,
> Her father killed it dead,
> And now it goes to school with her
> Between two hunks of bread. (*All laugh*).

INTERLOCUTOR: That scintillating comedian, our ebony-hued Mr. Tambo, will render a riot of risibility entitled *Nancy Fat*.

NANCY FAT

PIANO

O Nan - cy Fat she was a gal,

Fair and tall and slen - der, The fair - est gal I ev - er saw, In

all the fe - male gen - der, A love - ly foot I know she had, In-

CHORUS

to a boot to thrust, Her an-kles small were made for use, To keep from it tho dust. O Nan-cy Fat, What are you at, I love you as no oth-er, O Nan-cy Fat, Get out of that, With sweet-ness me you'll smoth-er.

116

A WORKING MODEL

O Nancy Fat she had a mouth, I cannot now describe it,
It opened like a safety valve, when she wished to divide it;
And well I knows she had a nose, and everybody knows it,
The end of it just looks as if the brandy bottle froze it. [*Chorus*]

O Nancy Fat had two such eyes, like burnt holes in a blanket,
The inspiration from her soul, I took it in and drank it;
She says this darkey am so sweet, she loves me like molasses;
Dat small machine she calls her heart, goes pit-pat as it passes.
　　[*Chorus*]

If Nancy Fat does marry me, how nice we'll live together,
She and I and all the bairns, like ducks in rainy weather;
And as we march unto de church, and hear de bells a-ringin',
De joy will break dis lubber's heart, to hear de darkies singin'. [*Chorus*]

INTERLOCUTOR: Say, Mr. Bones, what happened to that beautiful beard that you used to wear?

BONES: That full beard?

INTERLOCUTOR: Certainly, it was a full beard, and a very fine one.

BONES: Yes, that was a wonderful beard. It took me years to raise it.

INTERLOCUTOR: Then why didn't you keep it?

BONES: Well, I'll tell you. It was this way. The other day a friend of mine came up and he was admiring my beard. And he says to me, "Mr. Bones, what do you do at night with that beard? Do you sleep with it on the outside of the covers or the inside?" And I said I really didn't know exactly and I'd find out for him.

INTERLOCUTOR: Yes, yes, go on. What did you find?

BONES: Well, sir, I tried sleeping with it on the outside of the covers, and I couldn't go to sleep, and then I tried it on the inside and I couldn't go to sleep, and I tried it both ways some more, and still I couldn't go to sleep, and so the next day I shaved off the beard. (*All laugh.*)

INTERLOCUTOR: We will now have an instrumental number by the band, in the fascinating rhythm of *The Cake Walk*.

(The following number is a combination of three cake walks, *Little Alligator Bait*, *Chocolate* and *Eli Green's*, published by M. Witmark & Sons and the Edw. B. Marks Music Co., and used by their permission.)

CAKE WALK

PIANO

PIANO

"GENTLEMEN, BE SEATED!"

INTERLOCUTOR: By the way, Mr. Bones, what is a vacuum?

BONES: Why, I can't—er—er—describe it. I have it in my head.

INTERLOCUTOR: Say, what kind of music can you play on a shoe horn?

BONES: Footnotes.

INTERLOCUTOR: Where do you live now, Mr. Bones?

BONES: Swampscott.

INTERLOCUTOR: Isn't that the place where they ring curfew every night at eight?

BONES: They used to, but they don't any more.

INTERLOCUTOR: Why not?

BONES: Because they woke everybody up.

INTERLOCUTOR: And now, last but not least, what is your own personal definition of garlic?

BONES: Why, that's easy. Garlic is a vegetable limburger.

INTERLOCUTOR: When is a joke not a joke ?

BONES: Usually.

TAMBO: I can ask some riddles, too.

INTERLOCUTOR: Go ahead, Tambo. What riddles do you know?

TAMBO: When, oh, when will water stop running down hill?

INTERLOCUTOR: My dear man, water will never stop running down hill.

TAMBO: Oh, yes, it will. Water will stop running down hill when it gets to the bottom.

INTERLOCUTOR: Aren't you clever? Do you know any more like that?

TAMBO: Yes. What is it that the more you take from it, the larger it grows?

INTERLOCUTOR: Well, what is it?

TAMBO: A hole. Now *you* ask one.

INTERLOCUTOR: All right, then, what's the difference between a cat and a match?

A WORKING MODEL

BONES: I don' know, what is the difference between a cat and a match?

INTERLOCUTOR: Why, a cat lights on its feet, and a match lights on its head. (*Laugh*.)

BONES: Well, then, why is your hat like Saturday and Sunday?

INTERLOCUTOR: I haven't the slightest idea why my hat is like Saturday and Sunday. Why is it?

BONES: Because it's on a week end.

INTERLOCUTOR: That soothing lullaby, *Little Alabama Coon*, will be interpreted by our crooning melodist with the honeyed palate, assisted by the quartet.

(The melody of the chorus is a sufficient reminder of this well-known song published by the Edw. B. Marks Music Co., and quoted here by special permission.)

123

"GENTLEMEN, BE SEATED!"

INTERLOCUTOR: Tambo, do you know anything about astronomy?

TAMBO: I haven't met the lady in years.

INTERLOCUTOR: No, no. Astronomy is the study of the nebular hypothesis, the study of planets. For instance, do you know that the sun is so far away it would take two thousand years for a wireless message to reach there?

TAMBO: Maybe you better send a picture postcard.

INTERLOCUTOR: Good heavens, man, don't you realize that the sun is often at a distance of ninety-three million miles?

TAMBO: Oh, that must be out near New Rochelle!

INTERLOCUTOR: New Rochelle! Nothing of the kind. Don't you know that the sun gives us all our light?

TAMBO. Sun may give us our light, but I notice that the gas company makes us pay for it.

INTERLOCUTOR: Scientists have estimated the sun travels toward the earth with great velocity.

TAMBO: I used to ride one.

INTERLOCUTOR: I don't believe you know what velocity is.

TAMBO: Sure I do; it's a bicycle with three legs.

INTERLOCUTOR: Do you know that the sun gives us life?

TAMBO: That's nothing. I know a judge who gives us the same thing! . . . (*All laugh*.) Does anybody live up in the sun?

INTERLOCUTOR: I don't think so, because when you look at it through a telescope everything looks bare.

TAMBO: Then, maybe only women live there.

INTERLOCUTOR: No, no, all you can see in the sun is gas and hot air.

TAMBO: Oh, I see, they have policemen up there, too.

INTERLOCUTOR: I can see if you ever get on the police force it will be a miracle. Perhaps you don't even know what a miracle is.

TAMBO: Sure, I know what a miracle is.

A WORKING MODEL

INTERLOCUTOR: Very well, then, what is a miracle?

TAMBO: If you see a bull in a field, that's no miracle.

INTERLOCUTOR: Very true; if you see a bull in a field, that's no miracle.

TAMBO: If you see that bull eating a thistle, that's no miracle.

INTERLOCUTOR: Correct; that's no miracle.

TAMBO: If you see a little meadowlark singing while that bull is eating the thistle, that still ain't no miracle.

INTERLOCUTOR: Still that's no miracle.

TAMBO: But if you see that bull sitting on that thistle singing like that lark, man, that's a *miracle!*

INTERLOCUTOR: Ladies and Gentlemen, we will now close our minstrel show with the entire company singing, *Oh! Susanna.*

(*Oh! Susanna* is one of the catchiest of the Foster songs, and makes a splendid finish and "walk around.")

(If preferred, the chorus of *A Hot Time in the Old Town* may be used again as a closing number. A recent popular revival, also, is *Down South*, whose chorus is given herewith.)

Come on down south, way way down south, where
    the sun shines every day,
Soft skies of blue smile down on you, and all the
    birds are singing clear and gay.
Come on along, join in the song, jump on board, it
    won't be long,
We're on our way, hip, hip, hurray! We're going
    down south to-day!

OH! SUSANNA

"GENTLEMEN, BE SEATED!"

I jumped aboard de telegraph
   And travelled down de ribber,
De 'lectric fluid magnified,
   And killed five hundred nigger.
De bullgine bust, de horse runs off,
   I really thought I'd die;
I shut my eyes to hold my breath:
   Susanna, don't you cry.   [Chorus]

I had a dream the odder night,
   When eb'ry t'ing was still;
I thought I saw Susanna,
   A-coming down de hill.
De buckwheat cake war in her mouth,
   De tear was in her eye;
Says I, I'm coming from de South,
   Susanna, don't you cry.   [Chorus]

I soon will be in New Orleans
   And den I'll look all round,
And when I find Susanna,
   I'll fall upon the ground.
But if I do not find her,
   Dis darkie'll surely die;
And when I'm dead and buried,
   Susanna, don't you cry.   [Chorus]

THE OLIO—A STUMP SPEECH

While the olio is strictly the part of the stage devoted to individual acts, the term has come to mean that part of a minstrel show which divides the first from the second, permitting the introduction of such specialties as the talents of the company may provide. Dances and musical acts, instrumental solos, etc., can be introduced here.

A WORKING MODEL

But the typical feature of the old-time olio, often figuring also in the first part, is the stump speech. A practical example follows, from an actual collection of former days:

HISTORICAL REMINISCENCES

Ladies and Gentlemen:

I appear before you this evening in the garb of an orator, and to show you how much disturbance one man can cause in a multitude. I assemble myself before you this evening for the purpose of delivering a lecture on ancient and modern history; also to express my opinion on the stability of self-government. Now, in order that my lecture should be fully understood, I shall divide it into two parts; T-O-X-, two. The first part shall be as we ourselves, and the second part shall be the same thing exactly. Now, suppose a man comes up to me and says, or suppose a man came up to me and didn't say, still I should say he said so. But we are digressing. In looking at the financial resources of this country, we find we have money (to get). We have gold, silver, and greenbacks. There are various kinds of silver: We have German silver, silver silver—and—and—"Silver threads among the gold." Well, that don't make any difference. Greenbacks, however, are worth more than silver, more than gold. For instance, take a silver dollar (that is, if the man ain't looking: we come pretty near knowing how to do that). Take a silver dollar, put it in a pocket-book and allow it to remain there a week. Take it out; silver dollar, that's all. Mark the difference; take a dollar greenback, and put it in a pocketbook, and as soon as you do you double it. Allow it to remain there a week, take it out, and you find it in *creases!* Very well.

Where was New York thirty-seven thousand years ago? Echo answers, "Nobody." I'll tell you where it was: The Indian's wigwam was heard in the distance and the scalping-knife and thomas-hawk was buried in the briny deep—and—and— yet we were not happy. Oh, my tiresome hearers, let us look back into dim futurity, and if you will believe me, and a great many have done so (while under the influence of liquor), things are coming to a crisis.

As the poet says, "Oh-oh-oh-oh (never mind, he owes everybody); Oh, I feel as though I could sweep." Reform! We as constituents of our representatives, we find—we find—yes, that is if we're lucky to find. But before soaring into the regions of hyperbolic rhetoric, and descending into commonplace hyper-criticisms, which always characterizes inquisitorial verbosity. Who is there among us who isn't here? Let him speak and I'll have him on the police force in ten minutes. Reform emanating as it does from the broad principles of liberty, liberties which were inculcated by our fore-fathers, liberties—and yet how strange. This young man I speak of—— And in reviewing from an asteroid standpoint of political exegitical analysis (what's the matter, am I too much for you?), or abglutinating the polytechnical ectoblasts of homogeneous etticeticisms, you can't do it, it's impossible. Reform! Of course you don't know anything about it. Neither do I, so I'll explain it to you.

"GENTLEMEN, BE SEATED!"

Having discussed my historical subject so fully, I feel confident that there are none within hearing of my voice to-night who are not satisfied that at one time or another Chicago was discovered, and to my sorrow. I was in Chicago during the World's Fair, about three weeks, and I never want to see or hear of Chicago again. I wasn't there ten minutes when someone went through me and stole my pocket-book. A friend of mine was with me at the time; he said, "I tell you, when Gabriel blows his horn in Chicago he'll wake up many a sinner." I said, "Oh, no, Gabriel will never have a chance to blow his horn in Chicago." He said, "Why?" I said, "They'll steal it before he has a chance to blow it."

AN AFTERPIECE

For an afterpiece, any short play can be used, depending on the cast available. Herewith is presented an "Africanization" of the ancient English comedy. "Box and Cox," which has been the staple fare of amateur actors the world over. It is curious to note that Mr. Christy (whose eulogy of the play is printed in full) failed to eliminate many of the typically English turns of speech.

DAN BRYANT AND COOL BURGESS
Masters of the Grand Manner in Minstrelsy

EDWIN P. CHRISTY HIMSELF
PRESIDING OVER HIS IDEALIZED TROUPERS

BOX AND COX

In One Act

AFRICANIZED EXPRESSLY FOR
GEORGE CHRISTY
BY E. BYRON CHRISTY, ESQ.
With The Stage Business, Cast Of Characters, Relative Positions &c.

ORIGINAL CAST OF CHARACTERS

Whitewasher, who labours hard all day, ... Mr. George Christy,
Waiter in an all-night Restaurant, ... " S. A. Welles,
Landlady of Cheap Lodging Rooms, ... " N. Kneass.

EXITS AND ENTRANCES

R. *Right;* L. *Left;* R. D. *Right Door;* L. D. *Left Door;* S. E. *Second Entrance;* U. E. *Upper Entrance, Centre Door.*

RELATIVE POSITIONS

R. means *Right;* L. *Left;* C. *Centre;* R. C. *Right of Centre;* L. C. *Left of Centre.*

EDITORIAL PREFACE TO BOX AND COX

This piece was written in London, and played in this country, many years ago. After many "long runs" and enjoying great favour with the public in its primitive state, it was adapted to the *Ethiopian Stage,* for *George Christy's* company of Comedians, in this city, *George* himself enacting the part of *Cox;* while that of *Box* was performed by *S. A. Welles,* for many years a prominent member of *Christy's,* and other first class troupes. It is one of the very best Farces in the language, and abounds in all sorts of *ludicrous situations, grotesque positions,* and *mirth-provoking dialogue.* It is, moreover, peculiarly adapted to the wants of small companies, requiring but *three persons to fill the parts;* and in troupes where the *Dramatis Personæ* cannot be furnished for a large two act Drama or Farce, this piece will be found "just the cheese"—and especially when they cannot be spared in the Acts of a "second part" of a Minstrel performance. The two principal characters, *Box* and *Cox,* can be played by the "end or corner men" of any company—either travelling or located—and though they require some study to learn the business, &c., properly, and "get the fine points down," once committed and performed with ordinary ability, it is bound to "make a hit."

E. B. C.

133

"GENTLEMEN, BE SEATED!"

BOX AND COX

[SCENE—*A room poorly furnished—in the centre a bed with curtains closed—a table and a couple of chairs—a grate and chimney-piece. Cox, dressed with the exception of his coat, is looking at himself in a piece of looking-glass which he holds in his hand.*]

Cox: Well, I golly! Dat's a nice lookin' head to go to a ball wid! I went and gub dat darky free cents, jes to clip de dead ends off ob my har, and he's gone and mowed it off like de wool off ob a black sheep in sharin' time. Neber mind: I won't go to de ball to-night, but den I must go to work dis mornin', for I promised to hab dat whitewashin' job finished to-day, sure, and dat ole gemblem's mighty 'tickeler. [*Knock heard at the door.*] Hollo! Who dat? Come in.

[*Enter* AUNTY BOUNCER.]

AUNTY B: Good mornin', honey. I hope de skeeters or de bed-bugs didn't bite you las' night. Did you taste de sleep ob de bliss ob innocence, eh?

Cox: Well, not zackly. Dat bolster on de bed might do for some darkies' heads, but it won't suit dis child! To use a highfalutin' 'spression, Mrs. B., it's destitute ob feaders at each end, and ain't got none in de middle.

AUNTY B: Well, de lord a massy child, I spose you must hab anoder—anyting to accommerdate yer.

Cox: Tankee! Den jes' be good enuf to hole dis glass till I finish my toilet.

AUNTY B: Sartin, honey. [*Holds the glass while* Cox *ties his cravat.*] Why bress my soul, honey! Who cut your har?

Cox: Look here, old woman, jes' please keep your obserwations to yourself! Can't a gemblem git his har cut widout drawin' forf remarks from ebery consulting feminine darky dat he comes across? [*Puts on his coat.*] Now for de hat. [*Puts on his hat, which comes over his eyes*.] Well, dar, dat darky didn't take less dan a bushel ob wool off dis cocoanut! Dat hat yuster be too tight for me befo' I got my har cut. Neber mind, I'se got two or free more. [*Goes in, and returns with three more shocking bad hats, of every style and pattern, which he tries on one after the other, but they are all too big for him*.] Now, ain't dat too bad! Wot's de use ob a gemblem habin' half-a-dozen hats when he can't wear any ob 'em? Neber mind, I guess I can make dis one do by puttin' about five or six ole newspapers under de linin' ob it. [*Prepares a hat and puts it on his head*.] And now I'm off. But befo' I goes, ole woman, I'd jest like to draw your 'tention to de fact (widout any idee ob hurtin' your feelins,) dat de last peck ob coal dat I brought home goes away amazin' fast!

AUNTY B: De lord a massy, Mr. Cox!

COX: Yes, an' it ain't ony de coal—but dat two cent candle dat I bort free weeks ago, and a quarter pound ob sugar—de brown kind— and a box of locofoco matches—and a bottle of skeedam snaps wot I take for my cold—all dese tings hab got de consumption mighty bad, and is fallin' away as fast as possible!

AUNTY B: Goodness sakes, Mr. Cox! I hope you doesn't tink I'd steal yer fings, does yer?

COX: I don't fink nuffin' about it—I got nuffin' to say about it. I didn't say you stole de fings, but dar ain't nobody but you and de cat in de house, and I wants yer to understand dat I don't believe it's de cat, dat's what!

AUNTY B: I tink you's mighty 'tickeler dis ebenin'. Can't you find nuffin' else to grumble about?

COX: I ain't a-grumblin'—I don't want to grumble—you neber heard me grumble in your life! But I should like to know who it am dat fills dis ere room full ob smoke while I'se away tendin' to my occer-pation.

AUNTY B: Why, I spose de chimbley, de

COX: Oh! now look here, old woman, you can't come dat ober

me. Chimbleys don't smoke pipes. It's *terbaccer* smoke dat I smells. Does you smoke, aunty?

AUNTY B: No, sir, pon my word and sacred honour! Ainer, mainer, moner might. Hope may never stir if I do!

Cox: Well, den, what makes de smoke?

AUNTY B: Well, I suppose it must be de—ah, de what you call—de ah— Yes, I guess dat's wot it is.

Cox: Well, I don't know but wot dat am the reason, but it won't do for me. I must hab anoder one.

AUNTY B: Well, den, I spose it must be de genblem in de attic; he's all de time a-smokin', and I spose de fluvium wot rises 'bove the noxious fluids ob de atmosfear must cotch de smoke and fotch it down into de room.

Cox: I spose dat must be de same coloured man dat I see comin' up stars ebery time I go down?

AUNTY B: Why, yes; dat is, I—

Cox: He's a mighty gallus lookin' nigger! Seems to me ebery time I meet him, as if he was a gwine to ax me, if I wanted anyting. I guess he must be a waiter.

AUNTY B: Well, I b'leve he is in dat bisiness, and he's a mighty fine young man, too, at dat.

Cox: Well, good mornin', old woman.

AUNTY B: You'll be back at de time you always is, I spose?

Cox: Yes, 9 o'clock. Don't yer light my fire no more, does yer hear? I'll do it myself. And don't forgit de bolster; my head akes ebery time I tink ob it. [*Exit* L.]

AUNTY B: I golly, I's glad he's gone! I declar to goodness, I couldn't hardly keep myself up, I was so 'feared Mr. Box, de oder lodger, would come in 'fore he went out. It's a lucky ting for me dat dey've neber met in dis room togeder yet; but I guess dar ain't much danger ob it, for Mr. Box am away all night long to de i'ster cellar, and Cox am as busy as he can be all day whitewashin': so Box sleeps in de daytime, and Cox sleeps in de nite-time, and by dis means I hire de room to bof ob em and git double pay for it, and dey am a couple ob knownuffins—dey don't know nuffin' about it. Now I must put Mr. Cox's tings out ob Mr. Box's way. [*She takes the three hats and puts them away.*] Now, den, I must put de key where Mr. Cox allers finds it. [*Hangs the key on a nail.*] Now, den, I must make de bed. When I makes it for Mr. Cox I puts de head to de foot, and when I makes it for Mr. Box I puts de foot to de hed. [*Goes behind the curtain and seems to be making it, and then returns with an apology for a bolster in her hand.*] De idee ob anybody grumblin' at such a bolster as dat ar! I don't know what folks want, for my part. [*Disappears again behind the curtains.*]

Box [*Without*]: Look here, why don't you keep your own side ob de star-case, sar? [*Enters, and then puts his head out again, shouting apparently to somebody outside.*] De nex' time you run agin me comin' up stars, you'll get butted, see if you don't! Can't you go down widout takin' up bofe sides ob de stars at once?

Aunty B [*Coming from behind the curtains of the bed*]: Sakes alive! Mr. Box, what's de matter wid you, eh?

Box: You jes mind your own business, aunty, will you?

Aunty B: Goodness me! You's in a great temper dis mornin' bout somefin. Why, honey, you's almost pale in de face.

Box: Dat's kase I's bin doin a pale business all nite—servin de customers wid pale brandy, and emptyin' out pails of slops. I has to work mighty hard all night, I does.

Aunty B: Yes, but den you has all day to rest in.

Box [*Looking significantly at Aunty B*]: Well, I oughter hab, dat's a fac', for I pays for it. So if you's no dejections, I'll just remark dat your presence is obnoxious to me—I wants to go to bed.

Aunty B [*Going*]: De lord a massy, Mr. Box!

Box: Stop! What coloured man is dat wot I allers meet goin' down stars when I's a-comin' up, and comin' up when I's a-goin' down?

AUNTY B [*Confused*]: Oh, him—O, dat young gemblem—O, he's de pusson—de man dat lodges in de attic, he is.

BOX: Oh, he is, eh? Well, I tink he's a rader ord'nary lookin' nigger, if it wasn't for his hats. I meet him wid a different hat on most ebery day, and most all of em's got whitewash on. I guess he must foller de whitewashin' bisiness.

AUNTY B: Well, he does, child. And now I tink ob it, he inkwested me to tell you dat he wishes you wouldn't smoke kwite so much, cos de fumes ob dat rank pipe ob yours flies up into de attic, and interferes wid his smellin' propensities.

BOX: Did he? Well, den, you can tell de gemmen to cork up his nose or else git a room somewhar else!

AUNTY B [*Pathetically*]: Ah, now, Mr. Box, you don't want for me to lose a lodger, does yer?

BOX: No, not 'ticklarly; but you ain't a-gwine to put my pipe out, I tells yer dat.

AUNTY B: Well, Mr. Box, does yer want anyting more wid me?

BOX: No, mam! I've had too much of your company already. Vamoose!

AUNTY B: Well, I neber in all my born days! [*Goes out muttering to herself and slamming the door after her.*]

BOX: 'Stonishin', de trubble I allers hab to git rid ob dat ole wench! She knows I'm up all night, and yet she sticks by me in de daytime, and won't gib me no chance to sleep. Now lem me see; wonder if I better take a snooze 'fore I eat my breakfast, or take my breakfast before I eat a snooze—no, dat ain't it 'zactly—shall I swaller my snooze—tut, tut, wot's de matter wid dis ole hed? Neber mind, I'd got a bunch ob eels done up in a paper in my pocket, wot I bort at Caferine Market [*Takes out eels and lays them on the table.*] and a cent roll. Now de nex' ting is to light a fire. Whar dem locofoco matches? [*Looks on mantel-piece, takes a box, and opens it.*] Now, ain't dat too bad? I bort a hull box on'y free days ago, and now ebery one on 'em's gone but one! Dat ole wench steals ebery ting I lebe here. [*Takes a potato candlestick off the mantel-piece in which there is a very small piece of candle, and looks at it.*] Now look at dat candle! I neber burn no candle myself, but de candle goes! [*Lights the fire and takes down a gridiron which is hanging over the fireplace.*] Aunty Bouncer's bin a-usin' my gridiron! De las ting I cooked upon it was a porgie, and now it smells wery much like red herrins. [*Places the gridiron on the stove, and puts eels on to cook.*] Well dar, I'se so sleepy I kin hardly keep my eyes opin. If I on'y had somebody to tend dese eels, I'd take a snooze. [*Yawns.*] I b'lieve I must take a little snooze anyhow. Maybe I'll wake up in time to tend 'em. [*Lies on the bed, drawing the curtains close. After a short pause, enter* Cox *hurriedly.*]

Cox: Well, dar, I'd jes' as soon a-tort ob bein' struck by lightnin', as gettin' away from work to-day; but de ole gemman's got trubble in de fam'ly—one ob de children is lyin' at de point ob sickness wid de measles, and de child's moder am troubled wid de newrology, or de tick-dollar-owe, I don't 'zactly remember which, in de left shoulder blade, so de old gentlem sed I might put off de whitewashin' for to-day, and take a holliday. Now, how shall I spend de time? I don't know weder to go and dig for clams ober on Long Island, or to take a nickel's wuf ob steamboat down to Staten Island, and fish off de dock. But I must have my breakfas' fust, anyhow. I can't go widout my breakfas'. I bort a lot of sassengers at de Dutch butcher's and I guess I'll cook 'em. [*Lays sausages on the table.*] I golly I forgot de bread! How's I gwine to eat breakfas' widout bread? Hello! wot dis? A roll! Well, dat's lucky, anyhow! Now den, for de fire. Hello! [*Seeing the match-box on the table.*] Who bin touchin' dem matches? Why de box am empty, and I left one in it a hour ago, I'se sartin! Well dar [*observes the fire*], de fire am lighted! Whar's the gridiron! On de fire, by hookey! And wot dat on it? Eels! Well, now dat's cool in Aunty Bouncer, dat is. She ain't satisfied wid stealing all my per-visions, but she takes de last match to make a fire, and uses my gridiron to cook her breakfas' wid. I ain't a gwine to stand dat, nohow! Come out ob dat. [*Seizes the eels and places them on the table, and then puts his sausages on the gridiron, which he puts on the fire.*] Now den for my breakfas' tings. [*Takes key hung up, opens door, and goes out, slamming the door after him, with a loud noise, which has the effect of waking* Box *up.*]

Box [*Suddenly showing his head from behind the curtains*]: Come in, if it's you, Aunty Bouncer, you needn't be afraid. I wonder how long I've bin asleep! [*Suddenly recollecting.*] Hi, golly, de eels! [*Leaps off the bed and runs to the fire-place.*] Hello, wot dis! Sassengers! *Whose* sassengers, dat's de question? Aunty Bouncer's, I'll bet a hoss! If she tinks she's a-goin' to steal my matches and eberything else, and den cook her breakfast wid my fire, she's mistaken, dat's all. [*Takes sausages off the gridiron and throws them out of the window.*] So much for de ole woman's breakfast and now for my own. [*Puts the eels on the gridiron again.*] I might as well fix de breakfast tings. [*Goes to the mantel-piece, takes key off, and exits at* R. *slamming door after him.*]

Cox [*Putting his head in quickly at* L.]: Come in, come in! [*Enters with an apology for a tray, with a few dilapidated pieces of crockery thereon, which he sets down and then suddenly recollects the sausages.*] Hi! whah! de sassengers! [*Running to the fire-place.*] Hello! wot's dis? Dem eels again! de debil! I isn't gwine to stand dis nohow. [*Takes up eels, throws them out of the window, crosses the stage to pick up his tea-things which he had previously set down, and encounters* Box *coming from his cupboard with his tea-things. They walk down the centre of the stage together till they reach the foot lights, when* Cox *speaks.*] Who is you, coloured man?

Box: Dat's jes de berry question I was gwine to ax you. Who is you, sar?

Cox: Wot you want here?

Box: Dat's jest what I was gwine to ax you, too—wot does you want?

140

Cox [*Aside*]: It's de waiter [*sets tea-things down*].

Box [*Aside*]: It's de whitewasher [*sets the tea-things down also*].

Cox: Go to your attic whar yer belongs.

Box: *My* attic? Gess you better say *your* attic!

Cox: Waiter, lef my partment rite away—if you don't, does yer see dat bunch ob bones? [*Doubling up his fist.*]

Box: De nigger mus' be crazy! *Your apartment?* Gess you must mean *my* apartment, you igmerant whitewasher.

Cox: *Your* apartment! yah! yah! I like dat! Does yer see dat?

[*Produces a dirty paper from the leg of his boot after searching all his pockets.*] Dat's a resweet for de last week's rent.

Box [*Produces a similar paper and shakes it under* Cox's *nose*]: Well dar's one ob de same tings, too.

Cox [*Suddenly shouting*]: Fire!

Box: Murder!

Both: Aunty Bouncer! [*Each runs to the door calling.* Aunty Bouncer *runs in at door.*]

Aunty B: De lord a massy, gemmen, wot's de matter wid you? [*They both seize* Aunty *by the arm and drag her forward.*]

Box: Aunty, turn dat whitewasher out right away.

Cox: Luff dat waiter leabe dis 'stablishment, 'meejetly.

Aunty B [*Hesitating*]: Say, look here, gemmen.

Box: Wot you mean? [*Pulling her back again.*] Whose room am dis, dat's wot I want to know.

Cox: Yes, you bullet-head wench, whose room am dis?

Box: Doesn't dis room belong to me?

Aunty B: No!

Cox: Dar! does yer hear dat? It b'longs to me.

Aunty B: [*Sobbing*]: No, to tell de truf, coloured men, it belongs to *bofe* ob you.

Cox and Box: *Bofe* of us?

Aunty B: O, dear gemmen, you mustn't get mad at me for doin'

141

de best I could. You see de fact is, dis gemman [*pointing to* Box] on'y bein at home in de day time, and dat gemman [*pointing to* Cox] in de night time, I tort I might take de priblege till de little garret bed-room was ready—

Cox and Box [*Eagerly*]: When will de garret bedroom be ready?

Aunty B: Why, to-morrow, I s'pect.

Cox: I'll take it.

Box: So will I.

Aunty B: Why, gemmen, if you bofe take it, you might's well stay whar you is.

Box and Cox: Dat's a fact.

Cox: I spoke fust anyhow.

Box: Well, dar—dat's enuf. You kin hab the garret bedroom—now lebe.

Cox: Lebe!

Aunty B: Now don't kick up a plug muss, gemmen. You see dar yuster be a partition here.

Cox and Box: Den put it up.

Aunty B: Neber mind—you hold on, and I'll see if I can't fix de garret bedroom dis bery day. So don't fite. [*Exit.*]

[Cox *walks rapidly up and down the stage, while* Box *takes a seat by the table and watches him.*]

Cox: Nice business, dis 'ere.

Box: Say, coloured man, wat you tryin' to do, eh? Tryin' to walk a fousand miles in a fousand hours?

Cox: Black man, you's growin' sassy!

Box [*Rising and advancing*]: Is I? Look here, whitewasher, I want to ax you one question—kin you fite?

Cox: No!

Box [*Throwing himself in a fighting attitude*]: Can't yer? Well den, square yousef.

A WORKING MODEL

Cox: Look here, wot's de use ob our fightin' I ain't got nuffin' agin you.

Box: Neider hab I got anyfing agin you.

Cox: Well den let's make up.

Box: Nuff sed—gib us yer claw. [*They shake hands.*]

Cox: Does you sing, Mr. Box?

Box: Why no—de gal wot I paid my devours to—wot I was gwine to marry—she didn't like singing so I frowed my voice away and neber looked arter it since.

Cox [*Aside*]: Dat's berry strange! Jes ezactly de way wid me. [*Aloud.*] Look here, Box, wot was your gal's name?

Box: Penelope Ann Fergusson.

Cox: Wot! dat yuster make i'ster soup down by Caferine Market?

Box: De same.

Cox: Well, dat's de berry same gal I was gwine to marry!

Box: No!

Cox: Yes!

Box: Why didn't you marry her?

Cox: Case I got sick ob de bargain. Why didn't you marry her?

Box: For de berry same reason. I didn't like her neither, but I got rid ob her by killin' myself!

Cox [*Starting back*]: Why you ain't dead, is you?

Box [*Solemnly*]: Yes. Listen! Penelope Ann and me squirreled—I wanted a bowl ob clam soup on credit. She wouldn't let me hab it—I was a-bustin' wid indignation, and I frew it at her in big chunks, she retorted by frowin' a stew-pan at my head—I dodged the dangerous piece of property, rushed from her presence burnin' wid wengence, and made my way towards de ribber.

Cox: Well, I tink dat was de best way to put yousef out, if you was burnin'!

Box [*Without heeding the interruption*]: De nite was dark—dark as de despair which filled dis bozzom—but I rushed on widout tinkin' whar I was a-goin' till I tumbled ober a tar-barrel dat was lyin' on de worf, and nearly broke my shin. Smartin' wid de pain, I picked mysef up, rushed to de edge ob de dock—took off my coat and laid it down carful, den took off my hat and laid dat down carful—den I tried to think ob a prayer, but couldn't remember none—den I stooped ober to make de fatal plunge—grabbed hold ob my hat, put it onto my head and made tracks for home as fas' as possible. I took good car to lebe a letter in my pocket 'dressed to Penelope Ann, tellin' her dat I'd killed myself for her, and now she tinks me dead. And I'se so glad you'se a-gwine to marry her.

Cox: Me! I isn't a-gwine to marry her. I isn't got nuffin' to do wid her, she's yours.

Box: O, go long. How's she gwine to marry a dead man? I tell yer she's yours, and she's gwine to be here arter you by ten o'clock— Aunty Bouncer told me so.

Cox: Ten o'clock! [*Both pull out tin watches of huge dimensions.*] It on'y wants quarter ob an inch ob ten now. [*A knock at the door.*] Golly, dar she is, let's stand against de door. [*They place their backs against the door.*]

Aunty B. [*Without, and knocking*]: Mr. Cox! Mr. Cox!

Cox: I'b jest gone round de corner.

Box: So hab I.

Aunty B. Mr. Cox! [*Pushes at the door, which* Box *and* Cox *redouble their efforts to keep closed.*] Open de do'! It's on'y Aunty Bouncer!

Cox: Is you shur dar ain't anybody dar wid you?

Aunty B: Nobody 'tall—let me in. [*They admit her cautiously.*] Gentlemen, I'ze got some news for you. Penelope Ann Fergusson am married to Mr. Knox de boot black. [*Exit.*]

Cox [*In his excess of joy butting his head against the side scenes*]: Hurror! hurror! O, ain't I glad!

Box: Free cheers for Knox! Yah! yah! yah! [*They both dance around the stage.*]

144

A WORKING MODEL

AUNTY B [*Poking in her head*]: Gemmen, de garret bedroom's ready.

COX AND BOX: We don't want it, we'll keep de room we've got togeder.

[Cox *is about to embrace* Box *when he stops suddenly, seizes him by the hand and looks eagerly in his face.*]

COX: Excuse me, Box, but de more I gaze on dose features, de more I tink you is my long-lost brudder!

BOX: Dat's jes wot I was gwine to say mysef.

COX [*Eagerly*]: Tell me, has you got a clam shell mark on your left arm?

BOX: No!

COX: Neider had my brudder! And on your breast—

BOX: Is a mole!

COX: Ha! ha! My mole-marked brudder. But no—

BOX: He doubts. [*Tears open vest.*] B-e-h-o-l-d!

COX: 'Tis dar indeedy. Base fears begone! Ha! ha! Come to my arms, ha! ha!

[*Both rush into each other's arms* C.—AUNTY BOUNCER *enters* R. D. *surprised.*]

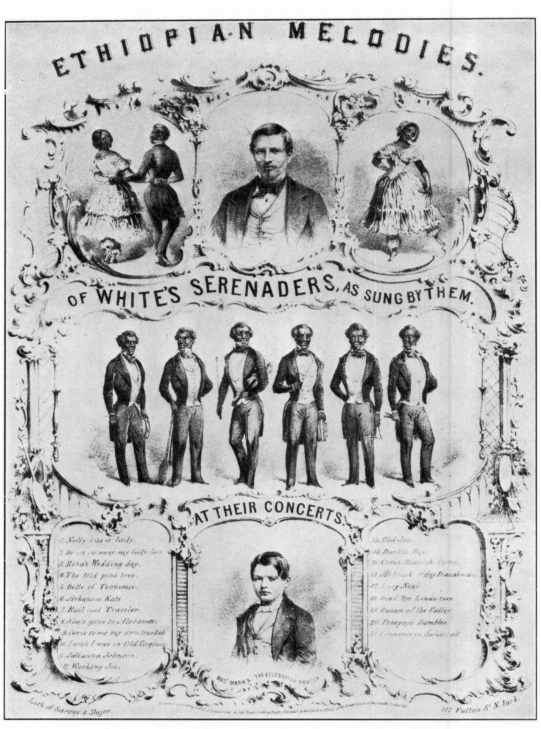

DANCERS AND INSTRUMENTALISTS
SPREAD ACROSS CHARLEY WHITE'S OWN TITLE PAGE

VIII. MINSTREL PRODUCING CENTRES

NEW YORK has always been, as it still is, the centre of the show business, and it produced its full share of resident minstrel troupes. But Philadelphia also was a prominent show-producing town in the old days, and boasted a permanent home of minstrelsy, the Eleventh Street Opera House, which lasted many years longer than any of New York's headquarters for black-face entertainment. In the normal order of consideration, however, New York comes first.

THE OLD-TIME RIALTO

Broadway then, as now, was the actor's stamping ground, except that its lower end was nearly two miles farther south than at present. That minstrelsy monopolized the efforts of a great many actors is shown by the records of the theatres housing black-face shows.

At 472 Broadway (between Grand and Broome streets) was located the most famous home of minstrelsy in the city, Mechanics Hall. Here Bryant's Minstrels, conducted by the Bryant brothers, Dan and Jerry, played continuously for more than nine years, from February 23, 1857, to June 2, 1866.

After seven or eight months' engagement in San Francisco, under the management of Tom Maguire, they returned to New York in May, 1868, and played nearly two years in a house later known as the Olympic Theatre. The last home of Bryant's Minstrels was on Twenty-third Street near Sixth Avenue, where they opened November 23, 1870, and continued until Dan Bryant's death in 1875. The record of about sixteen years in New York would be a significant one for any stock company. After the death of Dan Bryant, Jerry Bryant carried on with the show for some years more.

Another of the old-time minstrel houses was Wood's Minstrel Hall at 514 Broadway (near Broome Street). Wood and Fellowes' Minstrels were one of the first troupes in the New York field, their show opening in 1851 at 444 Broadway. Henry Wood allied himself with George Christy later, and played at 444 until the theatre burned in 1854. Then they moved up to 472 Broadway. For a time they ran two shows simultaneously, the theatre at 444 having been reopened. In 1857, they moved to the Marble Palace, 561–563 Broadway, where they remained for two years. Wood returned alone to 444, and there conducted minstrel shows for another three years. Another move took the company to Wood's Minstrel Hall, where it flourished until 1866. Fifteen years was Wood's record of dispensing minstrelsy as a steady diet to the theatregoers of the metropolis.

(Henry Wood, incidentally, was the brother of Fernando Wood, Mayor of New York during part of the Civil War years.)

The early records show also that George Christy's Minstrels held forth at Niblo's Saloon in April of 1860. In the list of players is the

BILLY BIRCH

name of W. Arlington, later to become famous as Billy Arlington, heading his own company, and also at one time a member of Billy Emerson's troupe, and associated with Leon, Kelly, Donniker, Cotton, and other outstanding minstrels.

The San Francisco Minstrels, originated by the famous quartet, Birch, Wambold, Bernard, and Backus (with Bernard later dropped from the firm), were for a long time residents of New York. Their location in 1865 was at 585 Broadway, which is described in the bills as being "opposite the St. Nicholas Hotel." Another bill, dated 1866, shows the San Franciscans still at the same theatre.

In the oldest playbills, 720 Broadway is shown as the uptown limit of the theatre district. Here stood the Waverly Theatre, near Waverly Place, where Kelly and Leon's Minstrels played a long engagement in the early '70's.

A few years later, the Rialto had been extended as far north as Twenty-third Street, with Bryant's Minstrels as the pioneers. In 1872, it had travelled five squares more, to Twenty-eighth Street, the new home of the San Francisco Minstrels.

The Palace of Music was occupied in 1862 by Campbell's Minstrels. It was on Fourteenth Street near Sixth Avenue, and was known as the Fourteenth Street Theatre. Campbell's

GEORGE CHRISTY

troupe stayed in this house for more than two years, then played at the People's Theatre for a year or two, and finally went under the R. M. Hooley banner.

By 1872, the theatre at 585 Broadway was called White's Athenæum, and was occupied by White's Minstrels. In the White Company were included such great favourites as Luke Schoolcraft and George E. Coes (who later headed minstrel troupes of their own) and the banjoist and singer, J. K. Campbell.

Charles T. White had first ventured into the minstrel field in New York when he established a theatre at 53 Bowery. He was burned out twice, but rebuilt each time. In 1854, he opened another theatre at 49 Bowery, and devoted it also to minstrelsy. Prices of admission were $6\frac{1}{4}$ and $12\frac{1}{2}$ cents! It was after his third fire on the Bowery that White finally moved to 585 Broadway.

Three big companies of minstrels were going at full blast in New York early in 1872, and toward the close of the year the number became four, with the advent of Emerson's California Minstrels, "T. Maguire and Billy Emerson, Props. and Managers."

A playbill dated March 12, 1877, shows the San Francisco Minstrels still in New York at the corner of Twenty-ninth Street and Broadway. In this bill are several famous names, besides those of Birch, Wambold, and Backus. The arrangement of the overture is credited to W. S. Mullaly, known in the show shops and in the music publishing houses of New York for many years as one of the most accomplished leaders and composers of the city.

H. W. Frillman, a famous bass singer, is in the list, as is the balladist, W. H. Hamilton. Bob Hart is featured as a comedy lecturer, and there is also the announcement of "the greatest of banjoists," E. M. Hall. (See p. 32.)

A playbill of Bryant's Opera House, dated June 27, 1874, announces a complimentary benefit to Nelse Seymour and Bob Hart, and the appearance in conjunction with Bryant's Minstrels of three star performers, Eph Horn, Charley White, and G. F. Browne.

Other minstrel artists of note taking part in the benefit were Dave Reed and the monologuist, Unsworth, billed as "the Black Demosthenes."

Another Bryant bill carries the note that *The Mulligan Guard* will be played by Bryant's band, "by permission of Harrigan and Hart." This famous song, written in 1873, is said to have "practically disrupted the amateur military organizations that had sprung up after the Civil War for purposes of politics or conviviality."

But the days of the continuous runs of minstrel shows were numbered, though several attempts were made in later years to establish a permanent home for minstrelsy in New York. The most successful of these was made by Lew Dockstader in 1886. For more than three years he held forth on Broadway, surrounded at all times by the brightest stars of the minstrel heaven, and the run was interrupted only by a cross-country tour to California.

The Youthful FRED STONE *(left) with his Father and Brother*

THE BRYANT BROTHERS, DAN AND JERRY

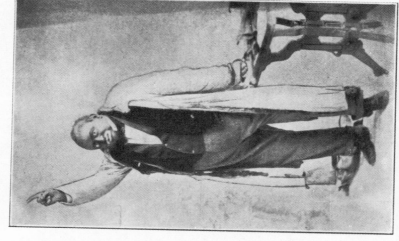

DAVID BELASCO as *"Uncle Tom"*

GEORGE COES

BILLY RICE, *Stump Speaker*

A GREAT INTERLOCUTOR, FLANKED BY TWO OTHER TYPES OF GENIUS

MINSTREL PRODUCING CENTRES

The '70's and '80's saw the organization of the great touring companies, each of which, however, appeared in New York for a few weeks or perhaps longer, as the metropolitan endorsement was thought necessary, as it is now, before a company took to the road.

Variety, afterward called vaudeville, and musical comedy began to have their innings, with the resulting curtailment of business for the straight minstrel show. The fact that actual females appeared in the musical shows created a competition that was fatal to the "all-man" performances of the minstrels. What chance did they have against the beauty, charm, and cleverness of Lillian Russell, or the snap, sauciness, and singing ability of Della Fox? Eventually came "The Black Crook," with chorus girls in tights, and New York's minstrel business abjectly gave up the ghost.

MINSTRELSY IN PHILADELPHIA

Sam S. Sanford built the first theatre in Philadelphia for the exclusive use of a minstrel show at Twelfth and Chestnut streets in August, 1853, and it was destroyed by fire the following December.

In April, 1855, Sanford's Minstrels opened at the Eleventh Street Opera House, and continued there until the spring of 1862. Sanford was one of the most famous minstrels of his day, and a pioneer in the business. He subsequently had other theatres in Philadelphia and one in Harrisburg, Pa., besides his interest in several travelling minstrel troupes.

Cool White was one of the star performers who marched under the Sanford banner for more than four years.

Bob Shepherd, another pioneer manager, opened a concert hall in the Quaker City, in 1856, and gave a variety show in which blackface artists played prominent parts.

Philadelphia's leading minstrel manager, however, was John L. Carncross, he of the fine tenor voice. He first appeared in Philadelphia, the city of his birth, with Sanford's company, in 1858, and continued with that organization for two years. In 1860, with Sam Sharpley, he organized Carncross and Sharpley's Minstrels and opened at the Continental Theatre, which was on the site of the present Casino. In 1862, the Carncross and Dixey Minstrels opened at the same house

SAM SHARPLEY

and played there for nine years. Both Carncross and Dixey retired several times, and in 1878 Dixey made his farewell final. But Carncross's Minstrels held on for eighteen more years, until January 25, 1896, when the veteran manager decided to call it a career. One of the young composers who wrote songs for Carncross and Dixey was John Philip Sousa.

Frank Dumont, who had long been a member of the Carncross company, eventually took charge of the famous Eleventh Street Opera House, whose record of continuous minstrelsy will probably stand forever unbeaten in this country.

The versatile Dumont was the minstrel model of the man who "in his time plays many parts." His first effort in black-face was as a ballad singer, when still a boy, with Arlington and Donniker's Minstrels. Later, he was with several companies as both performer and manager. For eleven years, he travelled with Duprez and Benedict's Minstrels, one of the most successful companies that ever took to the road. He sang with the San Francisco Minstrels in New York, and with Lew Dockstader's company. He was with Sweatnam's Minstrels in 1879, also as a balladist.

Minstrelsy is indebted to him for innumerable songs, sketches, and burlesques, a great many of which were produced by him with Carncross in Philadelphia, and later, when the theatre was under his own management. He was also a prolific contributor to the dramatic papers, particularly the New York *Clipper*, and was considered an authority on all matters pertaining to his profession.

Practically every minstrel man of note appeared at some time in Philadelphia's Eleventh Street Opera House.

E. N. Slocum, an interlocutor and actor of note, in association with Lew Simmons, opened a theatre in Philadelphia, the Arch Street Opera House, in 1870. This partnership continued for about seven years. In 1875, Willis P. Sweatnam joined the firm, and the next year Simmons and Slocum withdrew, and the company became Sweatnam's Minstrels. In 1886, however, Simmons and Slocum's Minstrels again occupied their old home in Philadelphia, with a revival of their former successes, while Sweatnam continued independently as actor and manager.

MINSTRELSY IN SAN FRANCISCO

In common with thousands of other adventurous spirits, the minstrel men started for the Pacific coast shortly after gold was discovered near Sutter's Mill, California. Perhaps the news had percolated to the East that a scratch company of minstrels was playing out there to "S.R.O." at five dollars a head.

In the minstrel record of San Francisco the name of Tom Maguire looms large. In 1850, he built the Jenny Lind Theatre, in which many stars appeared, until it was destroyed by fire.

Maguire brought George Christy and his company to San Francisco in 1858. It was Maguire who took Billy Emerson to the coast town in 1870, made him a partner, and called the company Emerson's California Minstrels, playing at Maguire's Opera House and later at the Alhambra on Bush Street. Previous to this he managed Birch, Wells & Soighter's Band in San Francisco for six years.

An Old Minstrel Circle, Its Stars and Its Headquarters

Maguire was also associated with R. H. Hooley and with "Colonel Jack" Haverly in later minstrel ventures.

Though the laurels that crowned the San Francisco Minstrels were mainly gathered in New York, the celebrated trio of Birch, Wambold, and Backus organized their company in San Francisco in 1864 and played there for nearly a year.

The Birch and Cotton Minstrels were organized in the same city in 1862. In 1886, these reunited old-timers played once more in the city that saw their first appearance.

THE GREAT EMERSON

To San Franciscans of the '70's and '80's, a minstrel show without Billy Emerson would have been "Hamlet" without the Danish Prince.

One writer on minstrelsy speaks of Emerson as "standing absolutely alone in his chosen profession; never before his advent had his equal been seen, nor will we ever again. The acme of versatility, the personification of grace, gifted with a voice an opera singer might have envied, and endowed with talents that are seldom given to man."

Another writer calls Emerson "No doubt the best minstrel that ever lived! Others could do things better than Emerson could; for instance, he was never so funny as Billy Manning, he could never do work just like Billy Sweatnam's, nor were his stump speeches as good as Billy Rice's, or even Hughie Dougherty's; but still he could do something of everything. As an end man and dancer he never had a superior and few equals, and who will ever forget his beautiful natural, rich, pathetic tenor voice?"

Billy Emerson carried such songs as *Love Among the Roses*, *The Yaller Gal That Looked at Me*, *Tassels on Her Boots*, *Mary Kelly's Beau*, and *Moriarity* around the world. He made everybody laugh with joy when he sang:

DAN EMMETT *at the time he wrote* Dixie *and in his closing days.*

BILLY EMERSON, *posing for his photographer and his* Big Sun Flower *public.*

MINSTREL PRODUCING CENTRES

"Oh, I feel just as happy as a big sunflower,
That nods and bends in the breezes;
For my heart is as light as the wind that blows
The leaves from off the treeses."

Emerson's first professional appearance was made with Joe Sweeney's Minstrels about 1850. He played the music halls for a number of years, and in 1864 was with Sanderson's Minstrels. In 1866, he made his first New York appearance at Pastor's Theatre. In 1868, Emerson, Allen, and Manning's Minstrels gave their initial performance in Brooklyn. Allen and Manning withdrew later, and in 1870 the first performance of Emerson's Minstrels was given. In November of the same year came the partnership with Maguire and the beginning of Emerson's great popularity in San Francisco.

Emerson made three trips to the Antipodes, the first in 1873, when he and his company scored a great success in Melbourne, Sydney, and other Australian cities.

Associated with him in San Francisco and his Australian trips at various times were many of the greatest men in the minstrel business, among them Bob Hart, Sweatnam, Lew Simmons, Kelly and Leon, Little Mac, "Add" Ryman, Carroll Johnson, Chauncey Olcott, Charlie Reed, and others. Reed was his partner also in the Standard Theatre, where three years of his career were spent.

Emerson made several fortunes, but poker, faro, the stock market, and the ponies took most of his money away from him.

He was with Hooley's Megatharian Minstrels for a season, and with Haverly's Minstrels when they opened in London in 1880. In 1888, he was in partnership with McNish, Johnson, and Slavin, returning later to San Francisco with his own company.

Emerson's career came to a close with his engagement by Wm. H. West's Minstrels. He died in Boston, February 22, 1902, and his body was taken to his beloved San Francisco, where it was cremated. His ashes rest in the Odd Fellows Cemetery, marked with a brass plate inscribed simply "William Emerson Redmond, 1846–1902."

The Howard Athenæum was for many years the home of minstrelsy in Boston. There the Morris Brothers, Lon and Billy, in conjunction with John Pell and J. T. Trowbridge, began to entertain the intellectuals in December, 1857.

Pell later died and Trowbridge retired from the business, but the Morris Brothers continued their activities in Boston and on the road. Charles Morris, another brother, was associated with the firm for a time, and later conducted a company of his own.

MINSTRELSY IN BROOKLYN

The name that stands out most prominently in connection with Brooklyn minstrelsy is that of Richard M. Hooley, he of the magnificent whiskers. All of his adult life he was associated with the best in the business, and he lived to be seventy-one. Born in Ireland, he left his home in 1844, and the next year was with E. P. Christy as leader.

In 1854, he organized a company with which he went to Europe and played in many of the Continental cities. During the '50's he was associated with the California manager, Maguire, in the management of George Christy's Minstrels. In 1861, he opened his famous minstrel hall in Brooklyn, and continued there for a number of years. About the same time, he ran a minstrel show in Philadelphia, and a little later he had still another show in Brooklyn. When this theatre was destroyed by fire, he put on a minstrel show at 201 Bowery, New York. In 1871, he invaded Chicago with a minstrel troupe and opened at a theatre later known as the Grand Opera House. After the big Chicago fire, Hooley built what was later known as Power's Theatre, and there his minstrel show flourished for about three years.

Following a road tour and the Brooklyn debut of Rice and Hooley's Minstrels (with Billy Rice, the famous stump speaker, as his partner), the minstrel impresario again went to Chicago with a company which occupied the Novelty Theatre for two years.

Other companies of ability and reputation tried at various times to become permanent institutions in Brooklyn; but none had the success that attended the Hooley organization.

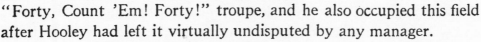

MINSTRELSY IN CHICAGO

The greatest name in minstrel management, however, in this country or anywhere else, is undoubtedly that of J. H. ("Col. Jack") Haverly. Chicago saw the inception of his most famous organization, Haverly's Mastodon Minstrels, the "Forty, Count 'Em! Forty!" troupe, and he also occupied this field after Hooley had left it virtually undisputed by any manager.

Haverly had been associated with other men in the management of minstrel troupes for twenty-four years before he organized the Mastodons.

His first venture was a variety house in Toledo, Ohio, and he assumed the management of Cal Wagner's Minstrels in 1870, but before this date he had managed Billy Arlington's Minstrels.

In 1873, Haverly's Minstrels took the road. One minstrel show was not enough for this energetic manager, for he in turn secured an interest in Tom Maguire's troupe, the Emerson Minstrels, gained control of the New Orleans Minstrels in 1876, and of Callender's Coloured Minstrels the year following.

In the meantime, he had bought the Adelphi Theatre in Chicago, the first of many that he ultimately owned or controlled.

Two years after the organization of the Mastodons, Haverly took them to London and played seventeen weeks at Her Majesty's Theatre, afterward touring the British Isles.

"GENTLEMEN, BE SEATED!"

At this time, the apex of Haverly's prosperity, he invaded Germany with his mastodonic organization and, in the words of Brander Matthews, "one result of his visit was probably still further to confuse the Teutonic misinformation about the American type, which seems often to be a curious composite photograph of the red men of Cooper, the black men of Mrs. Stowe, and the white men of Mark Twain and Bret Harte. It was reported at the time that another and more immediate result of this rash foray beyond the confines of the English-speaking race was that Haverly for a while was in danger of arrest by the police for the fraudulent attempt to deceive the German public, because he was pretending to present a company of *negro* minstrels, whereas his performers were actually white men."

Haverly's shows, sumptuously mounted and boasting the best known names in the profession, set a high mark for his competitors. But although he made a great deal of money in the course of his career, and was considered one of the best managers minstrelsy ever had, the end of his life found him in poverty, his last efforts in the show business having to do with a small museum in Brooklyn. He died in Salt Lake City, September 28, 1901.

IX. SOME OF THE ROAD SHOWS

HERE the name of Al G. Field heads all the rest. Minstrel shows equipped with stars who have loomed larger in the bills, shows with tremendously impressive names, shows claiming the ultimate in minstrelsy have come and gone; but the organization known as Al G. Field's Minstrels kept plugging away continuously from 1886 through the years. Though Field died, the big bills continued to carry his picture, captioned "The Dean of Minstrelsy," and every year the company was welcomed in towns throughout the United States.

Field was known as the "Millionaire Minstrel," indicating that he was a better business man than the average in his profession. He was also a very good performer, especially in monologues. His business experience was wide, for he not only filled executive positions with the Sells Circus, but was also associated with Duprez and Benedict's Minstrels, and Duprez was one of the cleverest business men in minstrelsy, a genius at advertising. It is claimed that Field was the first minstrel manager to carry entire stage settings and scenery, and also the first to build and operate a special train of cars for the accommodation of his troupe.

The company bearing his name was incorporated in 1910. A great many of the best-known performers were with the Field show at one time or other, among them Neil O'Brien, Eddie Fox, composer of *The Big Sunflower*, and Press Eldridge, one of the noted monologue artists of vaudeville. Eddie Cantor also served a black-face apprenticeship with Field's company.

"GENTLEMEN, BE SEATED!"

Hiram Patrick Henry wisely shortened his name to Hi Henry and became known as a good showman, as well as one of the best cornettists in the business. Hi Henry's Minstrels rambled from one end of the country to the other, visiting small towns and odd corners for a period of thirty years.

Hi himself was one of the big cards of his show. After the company had "made the parade," and stopped before the local hotel or theatre, Hi would electrify the crowd by "tripple-tonguing" a few tunes on his silver cornet, and the effect on the box-office was immediately evident.

A minstrel who headed a troupe which ran neck and neck with Hi Henry's in the race for popularity was "Happy" Cal Wagner. His Christian name was Calvin, but he easily sidestepped its connotation of strict and unbending religion. Cal was under the wing of Colonel Jack Haverly for a time, and was also associated with Ben Cotton in management, but through most of his show career he played a lone hand.

One of the biggest organizations of minstrels that ever took the road was that of Barlow, Wilson, Primrose, and West. All four of these men were performers of the first rank, each with a specialty of his own. Milt Barlow was noted for his faithful delineation of the old Southern darky; George Wilson was an eccentric low comedian and monologuist; Primrose was a singer, and one of the most graceful dancers that ever appeared in black-face; and Wm. H. West was a great clog dancer and show producer.

Primrose and West were partners for nearly thirty years. Their association with George Thatcher was also notable in its results, and after this alliance was ended, the Primrose and West Minstrels continued independently for more than nine years. At one time they had two companies on the road, Primrose heading one show and West the other. The long partnership came to an end in 1898. Then Primrose teamed with Dockstader as a partner for about four years, and

BILLY WEST

GEORGE PRIMROSE

One of the Greatest Minstrel Teams, on and off Stage

later headed another organization of his own, with occasional appearances in vaudeville.

George Wilson was one of the funniest comedians and monologue artists the minstrel stage ever saw, and, curiously enough, he was an Englishman by birth, though it seemed to be the very essence of American humour that he handed over the footlights. He came to this country early in life and appeared as a minstrel in San Francisco in the '6o's.

He attracted the attention of Haverly, and was with the "Forty, Count 'Em! Forty!" show for four years; then came his association with Barlow, Primrose, and West. Later, he and Barlow had a show, then Rankin became a partner, and finally George Wilson's Minstrels appeared and held the road for four years. He was with the Primrose and West show for five years more, and eventually appeared in vaudeville. Altogether, Wilson had one of the longest and most successful careers of any man in the history of black-face.

Long after the "Big Four" of minstrelsy came the "Big Three," Thatcher, Primrose, and West. George Thatcher's first important engagement was with Tony Pastor in New York. Then he went to Philadelphia as a member of the company headed by another Big Three, Simmons, Slocum, and Sweatnam. Then came three years with the San Francisco Minstrels in New York. A singer and a dancer, he claims to have been the first to introduce gags between the verses of his songs, a custom that many an entertainer adopted later. He was also famous as a monologue artist.

His first venture as a manager was with Ryman in Philadelphia, and shortly afterward George Thatcher's Minstrels played at the Arch Street Opera House in the same city. Thatcher joined forces with Primrose and West in 1882, and for seven years the Big Three toured the country with elaborate shows and a splendid array of black-face artists.

Thatcher's Minstrels took the road in 1890, and in three successive seasons he produced "Tuxedo," "Africa," and "About Gotham," all gorgeously mounted and widely popular.

George Thatcher played many vaudeville engagements singly and in association with other performers. A most capable actor, as well as a song, dance, and monologue artist, he appeared also as a Negro character delineator in two legitimate plays, "The County Chairman" and "Cameo Kirby."

Duprez and Benedict's Minstrels lasted for twenty years as a road attraction, although Benedict himself was a partner for only eleven years of that time. Charles H. Duprez has been mentioned as a business man of great astuteness. He had a Frenchman's talent for economy; he was a Parisian by birth, and he knew the value of advertising for attracting patronage.

At one time he possessed two Dalmatian coach dogs, then a rare breed in this country (covered with black spots on a white ground), and, with banners announcing Duprez and Benedict's Minstrels spread over them, they would walk the streets as a ballyhoo for the show. One of the stock sayings of the road was that Duprez wouldn't give anyone even a spot off one of his dogs.

The Arnold Brothers, at first two, Billy and Amos, joined later by another brother, Frank, were with the Haverly Mastodon Minstrels in Chicago, later with Hooley, and finally with Hooley and Rice. Billy Arnold's own minstrels were on the road for a number of years and gave a good show, for Billy was an unctuous comedian, and his "Billy's Dream" always scored. He was also the acknowledged tambourine champion of minstrelsy, and he always added excitement to the conclusion of the first part by spinning two tambourines at once.

M. B. Leavitt's name for many years was one of the best known in the show business. He was associated with both the stage and the business ends, and his affiliations were with many branches of entertainment such as Mme. Rentz's Female Minstrels, which subse-

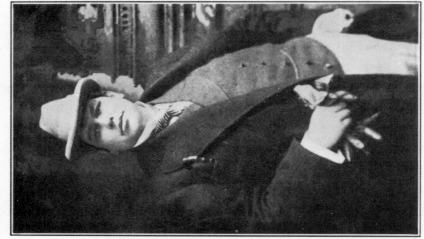

RICHARD JOSÉ

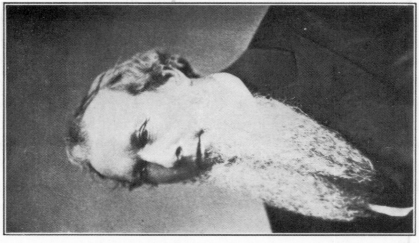

W. H. HOOLEY

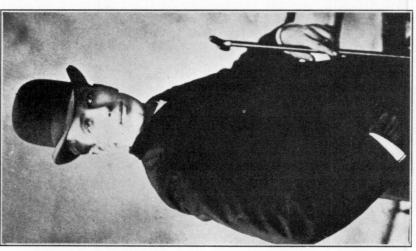

BARNEY FAGAN

A Dancing Director, a Manager, and a Singer of Note

quently developed into the Rentz-Santley Burlesque troupe. He sent
out a number of companies of Leavitt's Minstrels, among them Leavitt's "Gigantean" Minstrels, and a number of extravaganza companies, notably "The Twelve Temptations" and "The Spider and
the Fly." Leavitt was also the author of a book on show business which
is a mine of information.

McNish, Johnson, and Slavin headed a company that hopped
into the minstrel arena in 1885 and stayed there for more than three
years.

Frank McNish originated the act known as "silence and fun,"
which dozens of performers with some pantomimic ability have copied
since.

He served a long apprenticeship in minstrelsy before he became
a proprietor. His earlier bosses included Al G. Field, Hi Henry, and
Thatcher, Primrose, and West.

McNish was a nimble-footed dancer and could also sing, usually
crediting this ability to his experience as a plumber.

Bob Slavin died at the age of thirty-nine, and minstrelsy lost a
rare comedian. He was a great wit and an all-around entertainer, appearing with unqualified success in the Haverly show and with Emerson in San Francisco. He was also a member of the Howard Athenæum Company and the May Russell Burlesque Company. One
of his last engagements was with Wm. Henry Rice's World's Fair
Minstrels.

Sam Devere, banjoist extraordinary, won his popularity chiefly
through a famous ditty, *The Whistling Coon*, in which the audience
always joined. Starting in Brooklyn, going to Europe with Haverly,
and playing other variety and minstrel dates, he finally toured with
his own company in 1890, and though he played his last banjo solo in
1898, a company remained on the road with his name for a number of
years afterward.

Though Wm. S. Cleveland wound up his career as a booker of

169

SAM DEVERE

smalltime vaudeville acts, he was at one time a power in minstrelsy. He occupied managerial positions with McNish, Johnson, and Slavin, and became Haverly's partner in one of his ventures. About 1890, Cleveland had his own organization, known as Cleveland's Minstrels, and at times several companies bore his name.

After Haverly's death, John W. Vogel crowned himself "Minstrel King." He had managed a number of the big troupes, and was reckoned one of the best executives in the business. Vogel's Big City Minstrels toured for more than fourteen years. He also managed Al G. Field's show for seven years, and owned and managed the Afro-American Mastodon Minstrels and "Darkest Africa," both companies of coloured performers.

Cohan and Harris launched a big minstrel show in 1908, when the "Forty, Count 'Em! Forty!" slogan was discounted. They combed Broadway for talent, and found plenty of it, though it is a question whether the box-office ever justified the amount paid in salaries. At all events, the show did not break any records on the road. Later, however, George ("Honey Boy") Evans bought the show and reaped a small fortune from it. It was in this company that Raymond Hitchcock substituted temporarily for Evans, imitating even his make-up. (See pictures facing pp.170 and 230.)

The Gorman Brothers, James, John, and George, ran a minstrel show bearing their name for six seasons, from 1898 to 1904. They also appeared in white-face in various comedies, one of them being Marie Dressler's "Tilly's Nightmare."

AL. G. FIELD

RAYMOND HITCHCOCK

"HONEY BOY'S" PINCH-HITTER AND THE "MILLIONAIRE MINSTREL"

DANIEL FROHMAN

CHARLES FROHMAN

"COLONEL JACK" HAVERLY

THREE MANAGERS CLOSELY IDENTIFIED WITH MINSTRELSY

SOME OF THE ROAD SHOWS

"NOT COLOURED, BUT BORN THAT WAY"

Actual Negro performers began to come into the minstrel business in the early '70's. One of the first organizations of coloured minstrels was Callender's. The dean of the theatrical profession, Daniel Frohman, became their agent in 1874, and his brothers, Gustave and Charles, became the proprietors of the show in 1882. Charles Frohman was thus interested in minstrelsy long before he became America's leading producer of legitimate drama.

He was also advance man and treasurer of Haverly's Mastodon Minstrels at their inception in Chicago, and subsequently became Haverly's manager, continuing in this position until he and his brother Gustave took charge of Callender's Minstrels.[1] Richards and Pringle's Georgia Minstrels were another popular coloured troupe that toured for years. It was this organization that boasted as a member Billy Kersands, of the enormous mouth. Billy, it is claimed, could hide a billiard ball in one of his cheeks and go on and do his monologue without the slightest inconvenience. Curiously enough, the coloured minstrels applied burnt cork to their features, whether they needed it or not, and made up with as much care as did their white imitators.

Gus Hill managed an organization of coloured performers, of which the bright particular star was Ernest Hogan. He was the original singer of *My Gal Is a Highborn Lady*, one of the song hits of Barney Fagan.

Another historic combination was that of Williams and Walker, and the name of Bert Williams still represents the acme of Negro comedy and pathos. His singing of *Nobody* remains a unique achievement.

The team of Cole and Johnson is remembered with delight, particularly in such songs as *Under the Bamboo Tree*.

---

[1] An interesting relic of this association is a salary list, now in the possession of Dailey Paskman, showing that Charles Frohman was paid $15 and Chauncey Olcott $8.25 per week!

"GENTLEMEN, BE SEATED!"

The Negro performer has reached a prominence on the stage, in films, and on radio and television.

To the names of Sissle and Blake and Miller and Lyles has been added a whole tribe of jazz descendants of the minstrel tradition. J. Rosamond Johnson was a great name in the concert field, and the next generation brought such splendid Negro artists as Roland Hayes, Paul Robeson, Taylor Gordon and Julius Bledsoe, while Will Marion Cook, Harry Burleigh, R. Nathaniel Dett and others have given dignity and substance to the actual Negro music.

It is to the Negro that the white minstrel owes everything, for without the presence of the black race in this country American minstrelsy would never have existed. The pathos, the tragedy, the humour of the Negroes, their heritage of superstition and of religious fervour, their music, their linguistic whims and fancies, have been the richest material for translation to the stage, and minstrelsy took its toll of all these elements.

X. FAMOUS TEAMS OF MINSTRELSY

MCINTYRE AND HEATH

THE most famous team in the history of the black-face art is undoubtedly that of McIntyre and Heath, a contrasting pair of consistently funny effect. McIntyre is the lugubrious coloured man, who thinks that the silver lining of a cloud is probably lead, while Heath believes in fairies, a veritable Peter Pan, who knows positively that there is a pot of gold at the end of every rainbow.

It was in San Antonio, Texas, that they first doubled up in 1874, and so far as the records show, their association continued unbroken on the stage.

They played circus and variety engagements until the fall of 1878, when they organized McIntyre and Heath's Minstrels. Shortly after that, they appeared at Tony Pastor's Theatre in New York, where they were hailed with unbounded joy.

In 1880, they played with the comic opera prima donna, Alice Oates, in "Long Branch," and then toured again with their own minstrel show.

Hyde and Behman managed them for a season, and they went under the management of Primrose and West the following year, though retaining the name of McIntyre and Heath's Minstrels. Their most important minstrel engagement was with Lew Dockstader's Company in 1891. Later they played extended engagements with both Hyde and Behman's Company and the organization of Weber and Fields. It was with the latter that their famous "Georgia Minstrels" was produced at the Gaiety Theatre in Brooklyn in 1894.

They flitted between vaudeville and minstrelsy for seven or eight years, and in 1906 began their great starring engagement in "The Ham Tree," which they played for three seasons.

"In Hayti" was the title of their next show, another big success, but they will always be remembered most affectionately in connection with the immensely popular "Ham Tree."

The advent of McIntyre and Heath in the musical comedy field marked the beginning of the policy of featuring a black-face star which was later markedly successful with such men as Al Jolson and Eddie Cantor.

SCHOOLCRAFT AND COES

Luke Schoolcraft was a Southerner and had an opportunity to give the Negro character careful study; the results were later proved on the stage, although his early ambition was to be a Dutch comedian.

LUKE SCHOOLCRAFT

After two years of acting with Newcomb's and with Simmons and Slocum's Minstrels, he formed, in 1874, a partnership with George H. Coes, which was unbroken until Coes withdrew from the business in 1889.

This team appeared with a number of the leading minstrel companies, including one of their own. They were prominent in Emerson's Minstrels, with Hooley and Emerson, with Barlow, Wilson, Primrose, and West, and with the San Francisco Minstrels in New York.

Upon the dissolution of his partnership with Coes, Schoolcraft joined Dockstader's company in New York, his last minstrel engagement, for, after one sea-

Two Famous Teams of Black-Face Tradition

McIntyre *and* Heath *Entering the Field Vacated by* Delehanty *and* Hengler

The Song That Made Harrigan and Hart Irish

son with Dockstader, he joined the great troupe of specialty artists, Russell's Comedians, and played in "The City Directory" until his death, March 10, 1893.

Coes was a fine "straight man," had a resonant voice, and figured as interlocutor in many minstrel shows. He was also an excellent banjoist.

His first venture into minstrelsy was made in California, where he remained a few years. He joined Wood and Christy's Minstrels in New York in 1857. Again he went to California as a member of George Christy's Minstrels, and later headed a company in partnership with Sam Wells on the coast. Stock engagements and minstrelsy occupied Coes's time until he began the long partnership with Schoolcraft. He died in Cambridge, Massachusetts, in 1897.

DELEHANTY AND HENGLER

The writers on minstrelsy are unanimous in their praise of these minstrel and variety performers. One writer declares that they were "the greatest in their line that the world ever knew, or ever will know, in all possibility." Their first appearance in New York was with Kelly & Leon's Minstrels in 1867, which established them as favourites in the metropolis.

They not only played the best variety theatres, but were identified with a number of the foremost minstrel companies. They also toured in England and Ireland with pronounced success.

Delehanty composed many popular songs, in addition to his activities as a performer.

HARRIGAN AND HART

Though the principal fame of this brilliant team rests upon their long association before the New York public as delineators of Irish characters, they were originally black-face performers. They formed a partnership in 1871, and the next year appeared in Chicago with Arlington, Cotton, and Kemble's Minstrels. In later years, also, they resorted to burnt cork on a number of occasions. Tony Hart's reputation as a "gentle wench" has already been noted. Ned Harrigan was a great artist in both white and black-face. Their elaborate productions, unique in American history, unquestionably were a direct outgrowth of minstrelsy.

DELEHANTY AND HENGLER

MONTGOMERY AND STONE

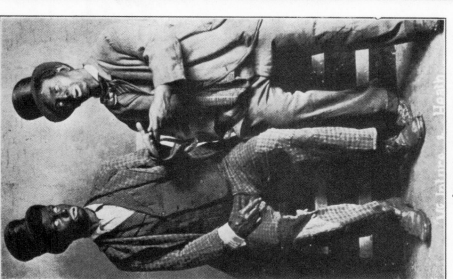

McINTYRE AND HEATH

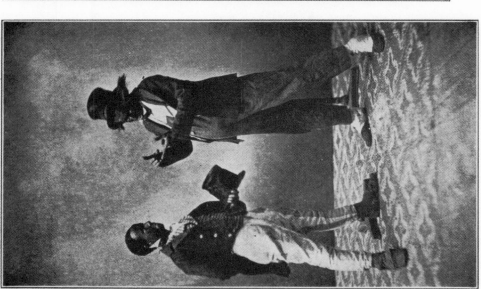

HARRIGAN AND HART

THREE FAMOUS MINSTREL TEAMS

All of these combinations eventually graduated from the burnt-cork circle, although the "Ham Tree" comedians remained permanently faithful to black-faces. Ed Harrigan lays down the law to Tony Hart in the immortal, "You 'spute me," McIntyre and Heath experiment with a little palm-reading, while Dave Montgomery already seems to suggest to Fred Stone the possibilities of straw men and other eccentric figures.

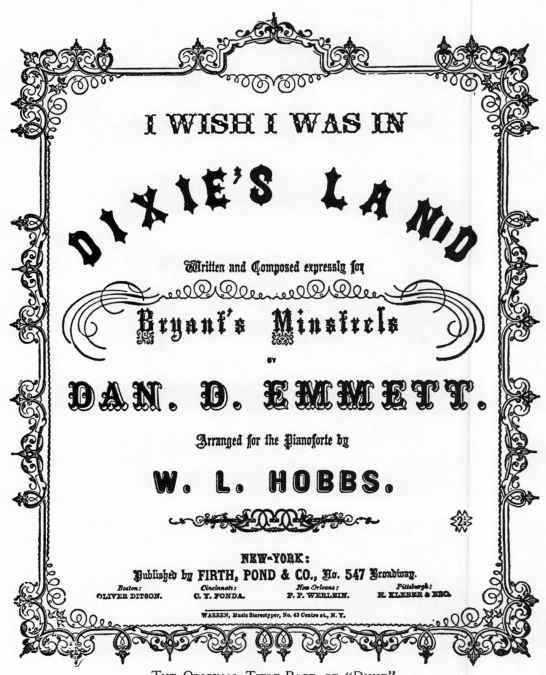

I WISH I WAS IN

DIXIE'S LAND

Written and Composed expressly for

Bryant's Minstrels

BY

DAN. D. EMMETT.

Arranged for the Pianoforte by

W. L. HOBBS.

NEW-YORK:
Published by FIRTH, POND & CO., No. 547 Broadway.

Boston: Cincinnati: New Orleans: Pittsburgh:
OLIVER DITSON.   C. Y. FONDA.   P. P. WERLEIN.   H. KLEBER & BRO.

WARREN, Music Stereotyper, No. 43 Centre st., N. Y.

THE ORIGINAL TITLE-PAGE OF "DIXIE"

182

XI. "DIXIE" AND OTHER EXHIBITS

ON A dull rainy Sunday in November, 1859, seated in his room in a boarding-house in New York, Daniel Decatur Emmett wrote a song that has set millions to marching and cheering. That song was *Dixie*.

Emmett, one of the original "Big Four," early in his minstrel career had begun to provide new tunes for the "essence" dancers, as the old ones became shop-worn. He was the composer of *Old Dan Tucker* and of the *Boatman's Dance, Walk Along, John, The Blue Tail Fly*, and *Early in the Morning*.

Dan Bryant needed a new "walk around" for his company, and asked Emmett to write one. *Dixie* was the result. Emmett did not write the song with any notion that it would become popular, but merely as a routine job for a regular minstrel performance.

"The song was introduced by Mrs. John Wood into a burlesque which she was playing in New Orleans just before the outbreak of the Civil War," writes Brander Matthews. "The sentiment and the tune took the fancy of the ardent Louisianians and they carried it with them into the Confederate Army, where it soon established itself as the war song of the South."

When Dan Emmett was a very old man, he toured the South with Al G. Field's Minstrels and received an ovation wherever he appeared.

According to Field himself:

Uncle Daniel was not in his best voice after he had marked his fourscore years, but every time he appeared before the footlights to sing *Dixie* the audience went wild.

It seemed as if they would raise the roof from the theatre. Every man, woman, and child would rise in a body and overwhelm "Uncle Dan" with applause. It brought back to the memory of the grizzled men who bore arms for the Southland the desolate camps, the fields of defeat, and the stirring recollections of victory. Those Confederate soldiers had sung it on the march and in camp. It recalled to the widows, wives, and daughters the occasions on which *Dixie* had been sung while the men were valorously fighting for the cause that was dear to all of them.

My acquaintance with Daniel Decatur Emmett, familiarly called "Uncle Dan," extended over thirty years. The earliest authentic announcement I have of his appearance as a performer is a bill which he gave me in 1897. The bill advertises a performance of the Cincinnati Circus in Charleston, S. C., on Nov. 2, 1841.

The song pirates were as active in the '60's as they have been ever since, and Emmett stated that, soon after his song had leaped to popularity, numerous persons laid claim to its authorship.

Some even went so far as to write different words to the popular melody, claiming the authorship of the original composition. Emmett had retained the original manuscript, however, and there has never been any real doubt as to the origin of the song.

Dan Emmett "hung up the fiddle and the bow" when he was almost ninety years of age. He lies buried in Mount Vernon, Ohio, near which town he was born and where he spent his last days.

His body "lies a-mouldering in the grave," but his song will go marching on through the ages.

Emmett also composed a comic song called *De Blue Tail Fly*, still with us, and full of real Negro atmosphere, and he is credited with the words of *The Fine Old Colored Gentleman* (with his name spelled "Emmit").

Jim Crow's Polka is notable both for its archaic musical form and for its references to the history and politics of its day. *The Other Side of Jordan* also touches upon political matters, with even more details of local colour, and really lands far away from the spiritual which it suggests. It was written by E. P. Christy.

Walk in the Parlour is true negro material, arranged by the same E. P. Christy, and bringing in some of the popular distortions of the Bible. E. W. Mackney, an early English exponent of black-face, wrote *Sally, Come Up* (under the undoubted influence of *Sally in Our Alley*) and also sang it regularly. He is credited with doing a "Jim Crow" in 1833.

DIXIE'S LAND.

I wish I was in de land ob cotton,
Cimmon seed 'an sandy bottom—

In Dixie's Land whar I was born in,
Early on one frosty mornin.

Chor.—Look away—look 'way—Dixie
Land.

Chorus—Den I wish I was in Dixie,
Hooray—Hooray !

In Dixie's Land we'll took our stand
To lib and die in Dixie.   (Repeat
Away—away down South in Dixie?

Old Missus Marry Will de weaber,
William was a gay deceaber;

Look away, etc.
When he put his arm around 'er,
He look as fierce as a forty pounder,

Look away, etc.
Chorus—Den I wish I was in Dixie, etc.

His face was sharp like bucher's cleaber
But dat didn't seem to grieb her;

Look away. etc.
Will run away—Missus took a decline, oh
Her face was de color ob bacon-rine-oh!

Look away, etc.
Chorus—Den I wish I was in Dixie, etc

How could she act such a foolish part,
As marry a man dat break her heart?

Look away, etc.
Chorus—Den I wish I was in Dixie, et

Here's a health to de next old Missus,
And all de galls dat wants to kiss us ;

Look away, etc.
Now if you want to dribe away sorrow,
Come and hear dis song to-morrow !

Look away, etc.
Chorus—Den I wish I was in Dixie, etc.

Sugar in de gourd and stonny batter,
De whites grow fat an de niggers fatter!

Look away, etc.
Den hoe it down and scratch your grab.
ble,
To Dixie's Land I'm bound to trabble,

Look away, etc.
Chorus—Den I wish I was in Dixie, etc

Hopkins, printer, 823 Tchoupitoula-
street, Now-Orleans.

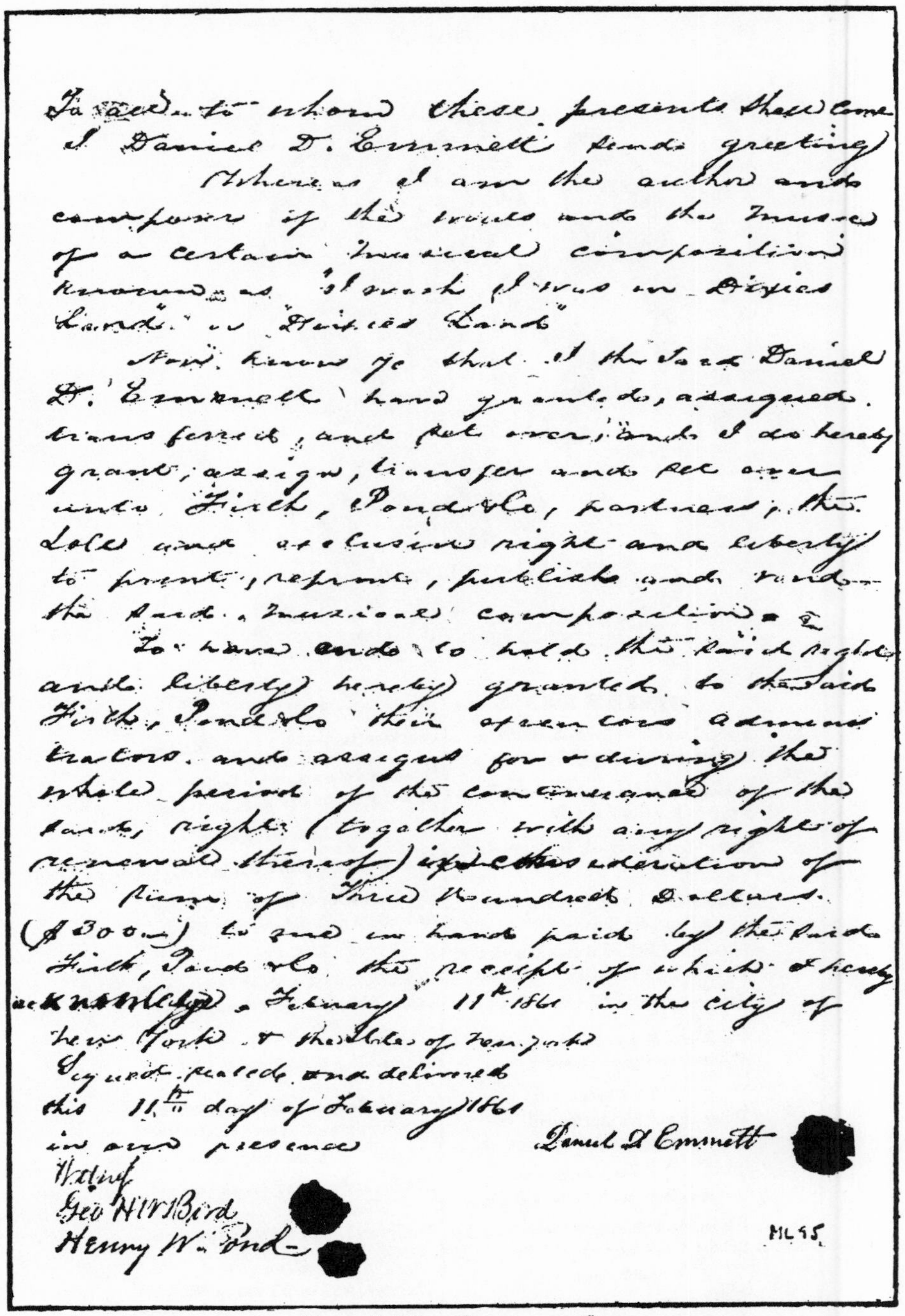
To all to whom these presents shall come
I Daniel D. Emmett sends greeting
Whereas I am the author and
composer of the words and the music
of a certain musical composition
known as "I wish I was in Dixie's
Land" or "Dixie's Land"

Now know ye that I the said Daniel
D. Emmett have granted, assigned,
transferred, and set over, and I do hereby
grant, assign, transfer and set over
unto Firth, Pond & Co, partners, the
sole and exclusive right and liberty
to print, reprint, publish and vend
the said musical composition.

To have and to hold the said right
and liberty hereby granted to the said
Firth, Pond & Co their executors adminis-
trators and assigns for & during the
whole period of the continuance of the
said right (together with any right of
renewal thereof) in consideration of
the sum of Three hundred Dollars
($300—) to me in hand paid by the said
Firth, Pond & Co. the receipt of which I hereby
acknowledge. February 11th 1861 in the city of
New York & the State of New York

Signed sealed and delivered
this 11th day of February 1861
in our presence

Daniel D. Emmett

Witness
Geo. W. Bird
Henry W. Pond

ML55

"DIXIE" WAS SOLD FOR $300

The Original Manuscript of "Dixie"

DE BLUE TAIL FLY

O when you come in sum-mer time,

To South Car-li-nar's sul-try clime,

If in de shade you chance to lie,

You'll soon find out de blue tail fly, An' scratch'im wid a bri-er too.

2. Dar's many kind ob dese here t'ings,
   From diff'rent sort ob insects springs;
   Some hatch in June, an' some July,
   But August fotches de blue tail fly,
       An' scratch 'im, etc.

3. When I was young, I used to wait
   On Massa's table an' hand de plate;
   I'd pass de bottle when he dry,
   An' brush away de blue tail fly,
       An' scratch 'im, etc.

4. Den after dinner Massa sleep,
   He bid me vigilance to keep;
   An' when he gwine to shut he eye,
   He tell me watch de blue tail fly,
       An' scratch 'im, etc.

5. When he ride in de afternoon,
   I foller wid a hickory broom;
   De pony being berry shy,
   When bitten by de blue tail fly,
       An' scratch 'im, etc.

6. One day he rode aroun' de farm,
   De flies so numerous did swarm;
   One chance to bite 'im on de thigh,
   De debble take dat blue tail fly,
       An' scratch 'im, etc.

7. De pony run, he hump, an' pitch,
   An' tumble massa in de ditch;

And died, an' de Jury wonder why,
De verdict was "de blue tail fly,"
   An' scratch 'im, etc.

8. Dey laid 'im under a 'simmon tree,
His epitaph am dar to see:
"Beneath dis stone I'm forced to lie,
All by de means ob de blue tail fly,"
   An' scratch 'im, etc.

9. Ole Massa's gone, now let him rest,
Dey say all t'ings am for de best;
I neber shall forget till de day I die,
Ole Massa an' de blue tail fly,
   An' scratch 'im, etc.

10. De hornet gets in your eyes an' nose,
De 'skeeter bites ye through your close,
De gallinipper sweeten high,
But wusser yet de blue tail fly,
   An' scratch 'im, etc.

The following song is perhaps the earliest musical celebration of a popular dance-form. It was years later that we had *See Me Dance the Polka,* although the current step was still the same.

Early in the Twentieth Century came a succession of dance-songs, with Von Tilzer's *Cubanola Glide* setting a syncopated pace. The *Turkey Trot, Grizzly Bear,* and *Bunny Hug* celebrated various stages of vulgarity at which Old Jim Crow himself would have opened his eyes in horror. (The original punctuation and spelling are retained in *Jim Crow's Polka.*)

JIM CROW'S POLKA

as dey star'd me in de face, Said he can dance the Pok-er.

CHORUS

Den up, and down,— fast, and slow, Toe and heel, It's

all de go; So if you wants to make a show, Why learn to dance the

Pok - er.

"DIXIE" AND OTHER EXHIBITS

Frue de kitchen I did ran,
I hide behind a frying pan,
And dis is de song dat I did sang,
Oh, I'd like to dance de Poker.
My lubly Rose I chanced to meet,
She took a squint down at my feet,
Says she dear Jim dem is complete,
      Den up and down, etc.

Says I dear Rose cum take a walk,
I want wid you to hab some talk,
Fust she squealed and den she squalled
You want to dance de Poker;
Oh, no, dear Rose, you is mistaken,
Now from your sleep you'se just awaken,
De nigger den, to sabe her bacon,
Began to dance de Poker.
      Den up and down, etc.

I tell you Rose dat is no go,
De way you does it isn't slow,
But Jim hab traveled, dat you know,
So drap down on dat Poker;
Ise got de news 'bout Mexico,
Dey t'aut to lick us at one blow,
But General Taylor wasn't slow,
To make dem dance de Poker.
      Den up and down, etc.

When General Taylor left his camp,
Provisions dey were getting cramped,

193

"GENTLEMEN, BE SEATED!"

To Isabel he took a tramp,
And landed safe as soda;
De Mexicans 8000 stand,
Dey crossed de ribber Riogrand,
Den blazed away at barrels of wind,
But found it was no Joker.
　　　Den up and down, etc.

De Mexicans dere plans laid well,
Dey hid demselves in de Chapparel,
But Rough and Ready made dem smell
Gunpowder a la poker;
One Mexican General, so 'tis said,
He got so skeared he swallowed his hed,
And three days after he was dead
He danced the Jim Crow Poker.
　　　Den up and down, etc.

THE OTHER SIDE OF JORDAN

194

Of all the ban-jo songs that have been sung of late, There is none that is now so oft-en call'd on;———— As the one I sing my-self and ap-ply it to the times: It's call'd, On the oth-er side of Jor-dan.————

"GENTLEMEN, BE SEATED!"

2. Around the Crystal Palace, there's a great many shows,
      Where all of the green ones are drawn in;
   There's snakes and alligators, mammoth mules and big potatoes,
      That were raised upon the other side of Jordan.
         I take off my coat, etc.

3. The *Sovereign of the Seas*, she went to Liverpool
      In less than fourteen days too, accordin';
   Johnny Bull, he wiped his eyes, and looked with surprise,
      At this clipper from the Yankee side of Jordan.
         I take off my coat, etc.

4. The ladies of England, have sent a big address,
      About Slavery and all its horrors, accordin',
   They had better look at home, to their own White Slaves,
      That are starving on the English side of Jordan.
         I take off my coat, etc.

5. The Duchess of Sutherland, she keeps the "Stafford House,"
      The place where the "Black Swan" is boarding,
   At a musical party, they asked for her a song,
      And she gave them—On the other side of Jordan.
         I take off my coat, etc.

6. They have got a "Bearded Lady," down at Barnum's show,
      And lots of pictures outside, accordin',
   She's going to take her eyelashes for a pair of moustaches,
      For to travel on the other side of Jordan.
         I take off my coat, etc.

7. There's the case of "Kosta," that has made so much talk,
      The Austrians, they tried for to maul him,

But Capt. Ingraham said, if they didn't let him go,
   He'd blow them on the other side of Jordan.
      I take off my coat, etc.

8. Our great father Washington, he was a mighty man,
   And all the Yankees do their fighting, accordin',
They will raise the flag of Freedom, wherever they can,
   Till they plant it, on the other side of Jordan.
      I take off my coat, etc.

9. And all the world must know, wherever we may go,
   Our Government will be ready in affordin'
Protection alike to all, both the great and small,
   That hail from the Yankee side of Jordan.
      I take off my coat, etc.

WALK IN THE PARLOUR

right from old Virginny, wid my head so full of knarledge, I nev-er went to free school, or

a - ny odd-er col-lege, But I will tell you one ting, It is a cer-tain fact I'll

git you 'scrip-tion of de world in a twinkling of a crack, So walk in, walk in,

walk in I say! Walk in-to de par-lor, and hear de ban-jo play.

"DIXIE" AND OTHER EXHIBITS

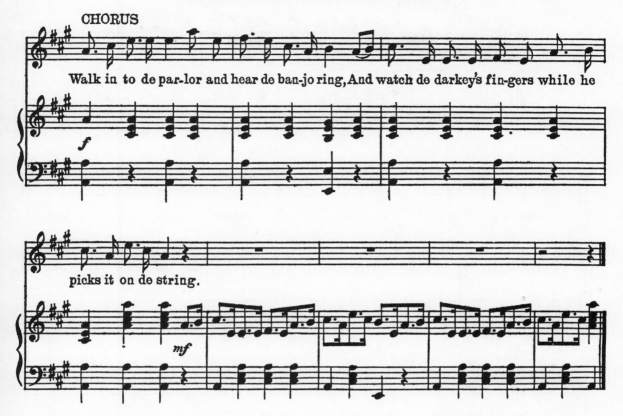

CHORUS

Walk in to de par-lor and hear de ban-jo ring, And watch de darkey's fin-gers while he

picks it on de string.

Lightning is a yaller gal who libs up in de clouds,
Thunder is a black man, and he can holler loud,
When he kisses Lightning, she darts up in a wonder,
He jumps up and grabs de clouds and dat's what makes it thunder.
      Walk in, etc.

Noah built de ark and filled it full of sassage,
All de odder animals took a cabin passage;
De elephant he cum last,—Noah said, "You's drunk"!
"No," says he, "it took me all dis time to pack away my trunk."
      Walk in, etc.

Oh, Noah sent de bird out, to look for dry land,
When he cum back, he had de banjo in his hand,
I took up de banjo, and played 'em dis 'ere tune,
All the animals, 'cept the elephant, fell into a swoon.
      Walk in, etc.

SALLY, COME UP!

Massas gone to town de news to hear, And he has left de o-ver-seer To look to all de nig-ras" here, While I make lub to Sal-ly.

She's such a belle, ____ A real dark swell, ____ She

dress so slick and looks so well, Dar's not a gal like Sal-ly!

CHORUS, *ad lib.*

Sal-ly, come up! oh, Sal-ly, go down! Sal-ly, come twist your heel a-round; De

old man he's gone down to town— Oh, Sal-ly, come down de mid-dle!

"GENTLEMEN, BE SEATED!"

2. Last Monday night I gave a ball,
   And I invite the nigras all,
   The thick, the thin, the short, the tall,
      But none came up to Sally!
   And at the ball
   She did lick 'em all;
   Black Sal was de fairest gal ob all—
      My lubly, charming Sally! [*Chorus*]

3. De fiddle was played by Pompey Jones,
   Uncle Ned he shook de bones,
   Joe played on de pine-stick stones;—
      But dey couldn't play to Sally!
   Old Dan Roe
   Played on de ole Banjo,
   Ginger Blue de big drum blew;
      But he couldn't blow like Sally! [*Chorus*]

4. Dar was dat lubly gal, Miss Fan,
   Wid a face as broad as a frying-pan;
   But Sally's is as broad again—
      Dar's not a face like Sally's!
   She's got a foot
   To full out de boot,
   So broad, so long, as a gum-tree root,
      Such a foot has Sally! [*Chorus*]

5. Sally can dance, Sally can sing,
   Dat cat-choker reel, and break-down fling;
   To get de nigras in a string,
      Dar's not a gal like Sally!

Tom, Sam, and Ned,
Dey often wish me dead;
To dem both all tree I said,
   Don't you wish you may get my Sally? [*Chorus*]

6. Sally has got a lubly nose,
   Flat across her face it grows,
   It sounds like t'under when it blows,
      Such a lubly nose has Sally!
   She can smell a rat,
   So mind what you're at;
   It's rader sharp although it's flat,
      Is the lubly nose ob Sally! [*Chorus*]

7. De oder night I said to she,
   "I'll hab you, if you'll hab me."
   "All right," says she, "I do agree";
      So I smash up wid Sally.
   She's rader dark,
   But quite up to de mark;
   Neber was such a gal for a lark,
      Such a clipper girl was Sally— [*Chorus*]

A Life by de Galley Fire is dated 1848. It contains some fine yodelling effects, and, with the curious *Eel Catcher's Glee*, represents a distinct departure from conventional minstrel material.

A LIFE BY DE GALLEY FIRE

cop-pers are boil-ing wild __ Who would not dis life ad - mire, __ it

zack-ly suits dis child __ I pine as I walk de street, like de fish wid-out a

fin, __ O get me my old ca - boose, where I lay back and grin. __

A life by de Gal - ley fire, __ where de cop-pers are boil-ing wild __ Who

would not dis life ad - mire ____ It zack - ly suits dis child. ____ It

suits,
it suits, it suits, it suits, it zack-ly suits dis child. It suits, it suits, it

It suits, It suits, it

suits, it suits, it zack-ly suits dis child. ____

suits, It suits,

Once more in de Galley I sit, Habanna Cigars I smoke,
Dere's many a colored Gal, in lub wid dis old cook;
    Habanna Cigars I smoke,
Dere's many a colored Gal, in lub wid dis old cook.
And wen de Captain's done, de basket I controls,
De wittels I serves out, to de poor and hungry souls. [*Chorus*]

O wen to de coop I go, de gobblers dey all look,
Becase dey know full well, dat I'm de slautering cook;
    De gobblers dey all look,
Becase dey know full well, dat I'm de slautering cook.
De chickens dey look in my face, and de duck dey wink dere eye,
Becase dey know full well, dat some ob de lot must die. [*Chorus*]

THE FINE OLD COLORED GENTLEMAN

fine old Color-'d Gem-man and dis nig-ra knows him well, Dey used to call him Sam-bo or some-thin near the same, De rea-son why da call dat was, be-case it was his name; For Sam-bo was a Gem-man, One of de old-est kind.

2. His temper was very mild when he was let alone,
   But when you get him dander up, he spunk to de backbone,
   He whale de sugar off ye by de double rule of three
   And whip his wate in wildcats, when he got on a spree,
   For Sambo was a Gemman, One of de oldest kind.

3. When dis nigra took a snooze, it was in a darky crowd,
   He used to keep them all awake, because he snored so loud,
   He drawed himself up in a knot, his knees did touch his chin,
   De bedbugs had to clar de track, when he stretched down his shin.
       For Sambo was, etc.

4. He had a good old banjo, so well he kept it strung,
   He used to sing the good old song of "go it while you're young,"
   He sung so long and sung so loud, he scared the pigs and goats,
   Because he took a pint of yeast to raise the highest notes. For, etc.

5. When dis nigra stood upright an' wasn't slantindicular
   He measured about 'leven feet, he wasn't ver' partic'lar,
   For he could jump, and run a race, and do a little hoppin',
   And when he got a-goin' fast, the devil couldn't stop 'im.
       For Sambo, etc.

6. Old Father Time kept rolling by and age grew on apace,
   The wool all dropt off from his head, and wrinkled was his face,
   He was de oldest nigra what lived on dat plantation,
   He didn't fear de debil den, nor all of his relation.   or, etc.

7. Old age came on, his teeth dropt out, it made no odds to him,
   He eat as many taters and he drank as many gin;
   He swallowed two small railroads wid a spoonful of ice cream,
   And a locomotive bulgine while dey blowin' off de steam.
       For Sambo, etc.

8. One bery windy morning dis good old nigra died,
   De nigra came from odder states and loud for joy dey cried;
   He layin' down upon a bench as strait as any post,
   De 'coons did roar, de 'possums howled when he gub up de ghost.
       For Sambo, etc.

9. De nigra held an inquest when dey heard of his death, ɪ,
   De verdict of de jury was, he died for want of breath;
   Dey went to work and skinned him and then they had it dried,
   And de head of dis here banjo is off dat old nigra hide. For, etc.

DE EEL CATCHER'S GLEE

Come dark-ies to de riv-er steal, A-way, A-way, A-way yah! While de night am dark as Din-ah's heel, A-way, A-way, A-way yah! Yah

hoo!   so spry-ly,   While de stars am peep-ing: We'll

grab de eels so sly-ly,   While de fish am sleep-ing.

Come wid your bobs an' eeltubs too,
    Away, Away, Away ah!
An' jump into de log canoe,
    Away, Away, Away ah!
We'll fish by de light ob de firefly,
    Away, Away, Away ah!
Dat wink his wing like Dinah's eye,
    Away, Away, Away ah!
Ya hoo! so sprightly we'll haul de sarpents up sa,
    An' den so slyly we'll fry de gals a supper.

Around de rod we'll make 'em spin,
   Away, Away, Away ah!
Like a cart-whip round a nigra's shin,
   Away, Away, Away ah!
Stop darky, what's dat make you shake?
   Away, Away, Away ah!
I'se got a *bite*—ob a *water snake!!!*
   Away, Away, Away ah!
Ya hoo! boys, quickly! De darky's looken blacker.
   Bind de wound up slickly, Wid a fresh chaw of tobacka.

Now take de sarpents from de tub,
   Away, Away, Away ah!
Each take his share home to his lub,
   Away, Away, Away ah!
Conumdrum! Why am we blacks religious say?
   Away, Away, Away ah!
Kase we're all an eeling [kneeling] for to *pray,*
   Away, Away, Away ah!
Ya hoo! so fly let blacks go possum stealing.
   Dar's none so spryly as dem dat go an eeling.

The minstrels often sang songs of the most maudlin sentimentality, similar to those which were in vogue during the mournful '90's. *A Lock of My Mother's Hair* is typical of early drawing rooms, but had its place also in the black crescent, when a sweet-voiced tenor or baritone decided to draw tears from his auditors for a change.

Found Dead in the Snow is even more melancholy, while a gentle touch of romance is wafted into noisy surroundings by the flowery words and music of *Had I the Wings of a Fairy Gay.*

A LOCK OF MY MOTHER'S HAIR

Ive a let-ter that was writ-ten long a-go, 'Tis a let-ter that I've treasured man-y

years; Oh! how of-ten I have read those fad-ing lines; And

o-ver them there's trac-es of my tears, ___ She sent to me her bless-ing in that

mis - sive,____ To see me was her con-stant ho - ly pray'r,____ The

dim. *rit.*

lit - tle lock of gray in this old let - ter,____ Is a lock of my an-gel moth-er's hair.____

colla voce *rit. e dim.* *pp*

CHORUS

I've a let - ter that was sent me long a - go, A

mf

let - ter that I keep with ten - der care,____ The lit - tle lock of gray in this old

let - ter,____ Is a lock of my an-gel moth-er's hair.____

216

"DIXIE" AND OTHER EXHIBITS

I've a letter that was written long ago,
    That was sent to me across the stormy sea,
When 'mong strangers I was wandering far away,
    And longing home again to ever be.
But underneath the sod my mother's sleeping,
    She's free from earthly trials and its care,
But ever next my heart I'll keep her letter,
    And the lock of my angel mother's hair. [*Chorus*]

FOUND DEAD IN THE SNOW

The snow had been fall-ing, and all thro' the night, The
tem-pest had raged in its fu-ry and might, The

217

sha - down of night were clear - ing a - way, But

bit - ter and cold came the dawn of day, A

lit - tle heart had ceased to beat, And

dead lay the or - phan in the street, No place but the snow to

rest his head, He was but a wand-'rer a - las, found dead.

Out in the snow, out in the snow,

Weep - ing, un - cared for, and no - where to go, Be-

numbed by the blast, he bowed his poor head,

In the cold morn-ing they found him dead.

Oh, the terror and pain of that night none can tell,
When, fainting with hunger and cold, he fell;
In vain he cried, "Mother," when dying he lay,
For no one was near when his soul passed away.
Poor little wanderer, none were there
To close his sad eyes, or hear his prayer;
No one to pity, no fond tear was shed
Over the wanderer, alas, found dead. [*Chorus*]

Oh, are there not many out in the bleak street,
Still wandering about in their cold bare feet?
Pray, turn not aside with glances of scorn,
Because they are poor and their garments are torn.
The orphaned poor, they pity need,
Withhold not compassion when they plead;
May it be thy joy and pleasure when old,
That thou hast saved many from hunger and cold.
    [*Chorus*]

The foregoing is an inevitable reminder of such other models
from the school of self-pity as *Little Barefoot*, and *Driven from Home*,
and *The Drunkard's Love Child*.

HAD I THE WINGS OF A FAIRY GAY

Oh! had I the wings of a fai - ry gay, I'd float with, the zeph-yrs a -

way a - way Or light - ly I'd skim o'er the o - cean blue In a

gos - sa-mer form of its own bright hue.

With a heart as light as a

sum - mer cloud, And a soul as free and a mind as proud As the

bound - less waste of the bri - ny sea, My glad-some my view - less

voy - age should be, Oh had I the wings of a fai - ry gay I'd

float with the zeph-yrs a - way a - way Or light-ly I'd skim o'er the

o - cean blue, In a gos - sa-mer form of its own bright hue.

cresc.

f

"GENTLEMEN, BE SEATED!"

From a flowery dell I'd swift emerge,
And hover in air on the mountains' verge,
Then cleave through the heavens afar, afar,
Till tranced in the light of a glittering star.
Through every region I'd take my flight,
And bound o'er the earth in a ray of light,
Or follow the storm midst the lightning's glare,
Then anon to some desert cave repair. [*Chorus*]

XII. CHARCOAL SKETCHES

LEW DOCKSTADER

THE name that looms largest in American minstrelsy and is best remembered by modern audiences is that of Lew Dockstader. When the minstrel business as a permanent institution began to decline in New York, it was Dockstader who kept it going to the bitter end, preserving the great traditions of the past and developing his own talents to the highest point.

Lew Dockstader's real name was George Alfred Clapp, and he was born in Hartford, Connecticut, August 7, 1856. It was after he had teamed with Charles Dockstader, and the combination became known as the Dockstader Brothers, black-face comedians, that Lew permanently adopted the name that became world famous in the field of minstrelsy.

Dockstader's first appearance in black-face was made in an amateur show in 1873, when he did a song and dance act with Frank Lawton in his home town. His cleverness attracted the attention of Harry Bloodgood, who added him to the troupe of Bloodgood's Comic Alliance, his first professional engagement.

Throughout his entire career, Dockstader never abandoned black-face for white,[1] as did so many of the other stars; he was a minstrel first and last, whether doing his famous monologues in a minstrel show, or headlining vaudeville bills throughout the country. His services were always in demand among the leading managers of minstrelsy when he was not heading his own companies.

After the termination of his managerial career in New York, he

---

[1] He did, however, show his versatility by playing Sir Joseph Porter in the Boston Theatre's revival of "Pinafore," to the surprise of even his staunch admirers, who had never thought of him as a legitimate actor. Dockstader's many accomplishments are still the talk of the theatre.

joined Primrose and West's Minstrels. Later, he again headed his own company and toured successfully for about four years.

Vaudeville then claimed him until 1898, when, with the help of George Primrose, another minstrel company was organized, bearing their names.

This company toured for five seasons, after which Dockstader once more entered vaudeville and continued in it until his show days were over.

J. P. Wilson, playwright, author, and lyric writer (responsible, incidentally, for the words of May Irwin's *Bully* song) supplies the following reminiscence of the great minstrel:

It was during one of Dockstader's vaudeville engagements that I first met him, when he was the big headliner over the Orpheum Circuit, and was booked to appear at the Orpheum Theatre in San Francisco. I had been house librettist for the Tivoli Opera House in that city and was called upon to furnish some material for the coming star in the way of extra verses for a topical song. I met Dockstader at the Baldwin Hotel on a Sunday morning, and found him a charming and courteous gentleman. One reason for his great popularity with the public was that he always handed out the latest gossip, the breeziest news of the day. He was always looking for material of the moment and of local interest in the city in which he was appearing, and often his hearers would exclaim, "How did he know that about so-and-so? He only came to town to-day!"

The answer is that he had scouts in every city he visited, ready to prime him with local gags that were right up to the minute.

I wrote him a couple of verses for *That Ain't No Lie*,[1] a song he was featuring, which went well, and also some parody verses on *A Hot Time in the Old Town*, besides providing various hints for his monologue. Lew's engagement was extended to three weeks, and he kept me under salary for the entire time.

---

[1]The verses were as follows:

Went to the roller rink for to skate,
Thought that to tumble would be my fate:
Stopped on the way to get a bracer of gin,
Took two or three before I went in.
Asked the skate man his skates for to try,
He looked at my feet and says he with a sigh,
"There ain' a skate big enough in the lot,"
Says I, "What's the matter with the skate I've got?"

[*Refrain:*] I'm a natural born skater, I'm a natural born skater,
A regular high roller, That ain't no lie.

Went down town for to cast my vote,
Thought I'd swap it for a two dollar note.
Man says, "I'll give you five, sure as fate,
If you'll vote the Democratic ticket straight."
I took the five, then another man
Give me ten to vote the Republican.
But to fool them both I couldn't resist,
An' I voted for a no-account Socialist.

[*Refrain:*] I'm a natural born grafter, I'm a natural born grafter,
I'se got my franchise, My vote comes high.

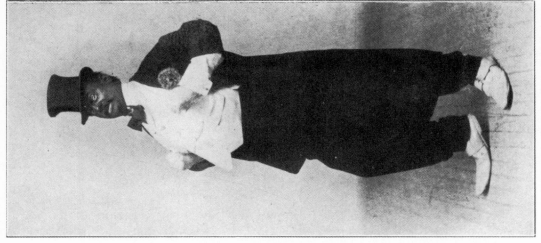

LEW DOCKSTADER

GEORGE "HONEY BOY" EVANS

THE THREE GRACES OF MINSTRELSY

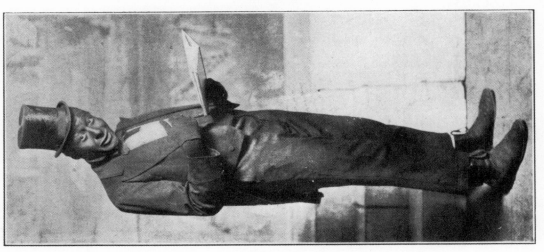

BERT WILLIAMS

"GENTLEMEN, BE SEATED!"

Josephine Sabel was on the bill the first two weeks, and among her numbers was the *Hot Time* as a straight song. Lew introduced the parody on the first night of his third week, with Miss Sabel sitting in a box watching the show. The burlesque of the singer, including her exit, was exceedingly funny, but evidently she did not feel flattered by the honour.

The gentle art of parody practically passed from the American stage with Lew Dockstader. In his death, minstrelsy lost its last and greatest true exponent, "a fellow of infinite wit, of most excellent fancy."

DICK JOSÉ

This tenor singer, best known for his interpretation of *Silver Threads Among the Gold*, was born in England, but has also been claimed by the Californians as a Native Son. They insist that he took the name of José from the town of San José in the Prune Belt.

Actually he came to America as an orphan boy, and first worked as a blacksmith in Reno, Nevada.

One of Richard J. José's biographers writes: "Never in the annals of minstrelsy has any singer met with more phenomenal success than that achieved by the subject of this sketch," which is not faint praise.

Dick's huge size and the volume and beauty of his voice made a real hit with Charlie Reed's Minstrels in San Francisco, with Lew Dockstader in New York, and with other troupes. He did the incidental singing in "The Old Homestead" for eight years and carried *Silver Threads Among the Gold, I Love You in the Same Old Way*, and other sentimental songs into all the big vaudeville houses in the country.

"PONY" MOORE

"Pony" Moore lived to be eighty-nine years of age, undaunted by his full name of George Washington Moore.

Circusman, expert "whip," driver of ten teams of horses simultaneously (hence the "Pony") he became in turn a minstrel end man, show manager, and father-in-law of Charlie Mitchell, one time heavyweight champion, defeated by John L. Sullivan in a historic ring battle.

"PONY" MOORE

"Pony" Moore was American born, but became an expatriate, living in England through most of his career. He was tremendously popular there, and seems to have started the English custom of laughing at American jokes.

Minstrelsy in England never recovered from the passing of "Pony" Moore.

GEORGE "HONEY BOY" EVANS

Wales preserved its tradition of song when it produced this golden-voiced minstrel, who was born in the little town of Pontytlin on the 10th of March, 1870. The spirits of the old Welsh bards, who hovered over his career, must have been amply satisfied with his success in his chosen profession.

George Evans wrote the song *I'll Be True to My Honey Boy*, and the name stuck to him through life. He first appeared as a minstrel with Haverly in Chicago, as a youth of twenty-one. The next year he joined Cleveland's troupe, and later he was with Primrose and West, then again with Haverly.

He graduated out of black-face into white in "The Good Old Summertime" and "The Runaways," musical comedies. "Honey Boy" Evans was featured in the big minstrel revival made by Cohan and Harris, and eventually became proprietor of the show, the youngest minstrel manager in the country. Vaudeville finally claimed him, as has been the case with so many minstrels.

EDDIE LEONARD

Eddie Leonard gave up his actual name, Lemuel J. Tuney, about the time he went into long trousers. Who can blame him? He soon made his alias famous as a "sweet singer," creating such song hits as *Roll Them Roley Boley Eyes,* etc.

Eddie Leonard headed his own minstrel show at one time but was remembered by another generation chiefly for his vaudeville triumphs.

AL JOLSON AND EDDIE CANTOR

Al Jolson, born Albert Joelson, sprang from Russian parentage and is said to be the actual hero of "The Jazz Singer," which he filmed in the early days. In any case, his father was a Rabbi. Jolson's first appearances were in 1903, in vaudeville, after which he joined Dockstader's Minstrels and then went back to the variety stage.

As a singer of "Mammy" songs and master of the "pep" technique, he achieved an almost unique reputation. The Shuberts starred him in their big musical shows, and he found a great measure of success in the movies.

Eddie Cantor built up a similar following, and his reputation also rested chiefly upon his highly individual work in black-face. He likewise belonged to the "pep" school, but had a smooth technique that was all his own, and made himself a legitimate musical comedy artist through such performances as "Kid Boots." Cantor was an outstanding star of the Ziegfeld Follies.

AL JOLSON

EDDIE CANTOR

STARS WHOSE FAME PRIMARILY RESTED ON BLACK-FACE

"GENTLEMEN, BE SEATED!"

"NOBODY" LIKE THE VERY LIKEABLE BERT WILLIAMS

One of the great character comedians ever to grace the American stage was Bert Williams.

Although he started his career in the early music halls, it was not until the year 1893 that he joined Martin and Seig Mastodon Minstrels in San Francisco, in which there were only five white men and five Negro men performers. It was this minstrel show that gave Bert Williams the opportunity to develop the talent that led him later to stardom in the Ziegfeld Follies.

In the early 1920's, this writer, then in his teeny-teens, met the already celebrated Bert Williams, who was appearing in the Ziegfeld Follies at the time when Victor Herbert, Rudolf Friml, Irving Berlin, George Gershwin, Gene Buck, Dave Stamper, and others were writing the music and songs for Mr. Ziegfeld's glorious shows.

Among the other composers mentioned here were Vincent Youmans and I, who were endeavoring to contribute musical and lyrical material for interpolation in the show.

Having met Bert Williams during one of my hangouts at the stage door of the New Amsterdam Theatre in New York, I was so impressed with his artistry that I was inspired to write something for the character he had made so famous with his rendition of the song *Nobody.*

As Mr. Williams came out of the stage door I approached him, saying that I had written a special piece of song material for him. Being the courteous gentleman that he always was, he invited me to have a drink with him at his favorite bar, which was in the Metropole Hotel just around the corner from the theatre. Mr. Williams ordered his "as usual" drink—Three Star Hennessy—and to be polite, I had the same. "Let me see your song," asked Mr. Williams. Whereupon I handed him the sheet of paper with the typed words.

BERT WILLIAMS

BERT WILLIAMS applying theatrical black grease paint to his face. Although this gentleman's skin was of a dark shade, "black-face" make-up was in keeping with the character.

He studied it for a few minutes and then began to recite the lyric. He got the feel of it and repeated the words in character. I cannot tell you the sensation it gave me to hear him speaking my words. It was the only time I ever heard my lyric delivered by Mr. Williams, because it did not get the chance to go into the Ziegfeld Follies. I have only the cherished memory of having heard the great Bert Williams interpret one of my lyrical creations, written for him to perform.

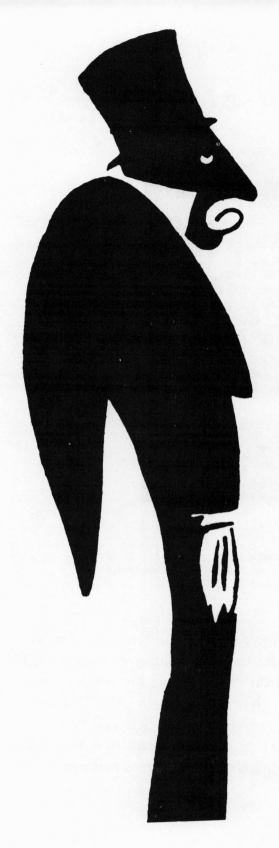

drawing by ALFRED FRUEH

NOBODY

Words by
ALEX ROGERS

Music by
BERT A. WILLIAMS

"GENTLEMEN, BE SEATED!"

BEN BECOMES BERT

Ben Vereen's re-creation of Bert Williams is the best ever given . . . nobody yet has matched it. Since it is a well-known saying that "Imitation is the sincerest form of flattery," Ben Vereen has paid the truest homage to an otherwise incomparable fellow artist.

So genuine is this re-creation that Vereen has gone to the extent of applying theatrical black grease paint on his face as Bert Williams did in the make-up of the character he portrayed.

Each new generation produces a young talent who becomes a celebrated artist in the years of his or her career. One of exceptional talent in this new generation is Ben Vereen. A young man, he has already established himself as an outstanding performer.

Born in Miami, Florida, and raised in Brooklyn, twenty-nine-year-old Ben Vereen has been lauded for his exceptional performances on Broadway as Judas in "Jesus Christ Superstar" (for which he received a Tony nomination) and for his leading role in "Pippin," which won him a Tony. His films include "Golden Boy" and "Funny Lady." His re-creation of Bert Williams in his nightclub act has won him widespread acclaim.

BEN VEREEN *applying the theatrical black grease paint in emulating the* BERT WILLIAMS *character.*

BEN VEREEN *made up in black-face for the* BERT WILLIAMS *impersonation.*

CHARCOAL SKETCHES

SCOTT JOPLIN REVISITED

Ragtime Music that was introduced and performed originally in the American Minstrel Show is not only enjoyed by a vast number of Americans, but is a favorite kind of music with many people in all parts of the world. One of the really great composers of Ragtime Music, rightfully referred to as "The King of Ragtime," was Scott Joplin.

Today his compositions are being rediscovered and are finding their way into the category of classical music. Concerts in the great symphony halls, such as New York's Carnegie Hall and Philharmonic Hall at Lincoln Center, and other showplaces of celebrated musicians, have included Scott Joplin's works—particularly *The Entertainer*, *The Maple Leaf Rag*, and the ragtime opera, *Treemonisha* —in their repertoires, along with Bach, Beethoven, Mozart, and the other great masters.

Scott Joplin was an extraordinarily talented composer and musician. He came from a musical family—his father was a natural violinist, and his mother possessed an exceptionally fine voice, so it can be said that Scott Joplin came by his musical gift honestly, from the very roots of folklore heritage.

Joplin wrote more than fifty ragtime piano pieces, marches, and waltzes. His influence is barely able to be contained. It crosses musical lines and cultural boundaries that Joplin could not possibly have foreseen. Harold C. Schonberg, in *The New York Times* of April 29, 1975, writing about Rudolf Serkin's performance of Beethoven's Piano Concerto Number One at Lincoln Center, conducted by Eugene Ormandy, said: "He played the A minor section of the Rondo with a real Scott Joplin left hand. It was big, brash, bouncy and fun."

The music world is now becoming aware of Scott Joplin's great musical output, and not only of piano rags. He is being recognized as the composer of at least one significant opera, *Treemonisha*, which has received critical acclaim with its first full professional production on May 23, 1975, by the Houston (Texas) Grand Opera, and later in New York City.

Gunther Schuller, the president of the New England Conservatory, made a new orchestration of the score for its premiere in Houston, and the music critics proclaimed this work a classic. The original orchestration, if it ever existed at all, was lost after Joplin's death in 1917.

The wonder of it is that Joplin, who was affectionately named "The King of Ragtime," could have written a work on such a high musical level: a three-act grand opera by an itinerant pianist and sometime cornet player, working on the midwestern vaudeville-honky-tonk-bordello circuit, born of an ex-slave in Texarkana, Texas, in 1868.

Although the opera was completed in 1911, it was not until 1915 that Joplin was finally able to arrange a backer's audition in a Harlem rehearsal hall, with no orchestra and only the composer at the piano. The audition was an attempt to attract financial support for a production, but to no avail. It was unheard of to find "angels" to back an opera with a Negro theme and black cast.

Despite the success of *Maple Leaf Rag* (the first great sheet music best seller in American popular music), Joplin died impoverished, his spirit broken, his energies spent on frustrated attempts to get his favorite musical brainchild published and performed.

But now, more than 60 years after Scott Joplin's death, this singular folk opera *Treemonisha* may, in time, become another American musical treasure alongside George Gershwin's *Porgy and Bess.* "Nothing quite like 'Treemonisha' has even been attempted by an American opera composer," said Peter G. Davis in *The New York Times*, "and its appealing naivete arises directly from Joplin's special personality and experience: to dwell on its flaws is rather like criticizing the markings on a butterfly."

Robert Jones in the *Daily News* of New York said this: 'Treemonisha' is a folk tale about a liberated lady who leads her people

SCOTT JOPLIN
King of Ragtime

out of superstition into enlightenment. There are some knockout ragtime scenes, but most of the opera is quietly simple, with a naivete
possible only to a very sophisticated composer. It bubbles with melody and it contains two of the greatest show-stoppers in theater history: the second finale ("Aunt Dinah Has Blowed De Horn") and the
third finale ("A Real Slow Drag"). In Houston, nobody applauded,
they just yelled. Some even lost control and dashed onto the stage to
join in."

PRICE 50¢

SEDALIA, Mo.
PUBLISHED BY
JOHN STARK & SON.

PERMISSION TO USE THE ABOVE PICTURE KINDLY GRANTED BY THE AMERICAN TOBACCO CO. MANUFACTURERS
OF OLD VIRGINIA CHEROOTS, BY WHOM IT IS COPYRIGHTED.

MAPLE LEAF RAG
(1899)

The Maple Leaf Rag *became the biggest hit* SCOTT JOPLIN *had ever written and the first great sheet music "best-seller" in America. Truly a classic ragtime piece, this selection prompted the lovers of his music to name him "The King of Ragtime." It is as popular today as it was in 1899 when* JOPLIN *composed it.*

MAPLE LEAF RAG.

BY SCOTT JOPLIN.

Tempo di marcia.

MAPLE LEAF RAG—The original publication of the composition in 1899.

THE ENTERTAINER

This composition of A Rag Time Two Step contains some of SCOTT JOPLIN'S most memorable rhythmic melodies. It now enjoys a worldwide revival (in 1974) as a featured piece of music in the Academy Award-winning motion picture, "The Sting."

THE ENTERTAINER.

A RAG TIME TWO STEP.

INTRO:

Not fast.

BY SCOTT JOPLIN.

10 — 4

THE ENTERTAINER—The original publication of the composition in 1902.

"GENTLEMEN, BE SEATED!"

THE VERY LAST IN THE EVOLUTION OF MINSTRELSY

MICKEY ROONEY *and* JUDY GARLAND *pass out the burnt cork to fellow performers* RICHARD QUINE *and* ANNIE ROONEY *before the shooting of their minstrel show finale in MGM's "Babes on Broadway," directed by* BUSBY BERKELEY.

JUDY, *in a brush with black-face.*

CHARCOAL SKETCHES

Courtesy MGM

The book you have in your hands is the one that inspired this scene. It's the scene now charming audiences in the current film "That's Entertainment." It just may be the Ultimate Stage in the evolution of minstrelsy.

Courtesy MGM

BUSBY BERKELEY is high in the air next to the camera. JUDY and MICKEY, the "end men," are down front. The music that was recorded the day before is played back to the company through a loudspeaker.

ANOTHER STAGE IN THE EVOLUTION OF MINSTRELSY

Reborn at the microphone, and revived in the modern theatre, the Radio Minstrels preserved the traditions in glorified style.

XIII. EPILOGUE

THERE are many other names that will occur to those who are still interested in minstrelsy and who once followed its astonishing history, year after year. It is impossible even to mention in these pages all those who contributed to this typically American form of entertainment.

Necessarily, also, the treatment of facts, figures, and personalities has been brief, with merely a hint of the range and significance of minstrel activities during the latter half of the past century.

No modern runs of plays, musical shows, or even stock companies can compare with the drawing powers of the old minstrel troupes. It was a hardy art form, and it is not likely that it will ever die, for to-day it still suggests the logical type of entertainment for amateurs, and its popularity over the radio has contributed to a revival that may actually prove permanent.

Aside from the competition of "mixed" shows, it is quite likely that American minstrelsy declined because of its overelaboration. When the settings began to look like a Drury Lane pantomime and the men dressed like gorgeous courtiers in a magnificent kingdom, not to speak of the increasing tendency to substitute white faces for black, the minstrel show began to lose some of its distinctive flavour. It could not compete on the same plane with the grandeur of the modern musical comedies and revues. But, left to itself, with its individual technique and its familiar formulas of wit and sentiment, all based upon homely realities of human experience, the minstrel show might well prosper again.

Let a company of good singers and dancers black up in the

old-fashioned way, crack a few jokes of naïve simplicity, and present some straightforward numbers of immediate appeal, and they will be fairly sure of finding an audience at any time.

This book is presented not as an obituary to minstrelsy, but as an advance notice of its permanent life.

INDEX

Songs With Words and Music

Words of Songs

(without printed music)

INDEX

References to Songs

Barefoot, Little, 220
Big Sun Flower, The, 33, 34, 159
Blue Tail Fly, 173, 184, 188
Boatman's Dance, 172
Bunny Hug, 190

Clar de Kitchen, 13
Cubanola Glide, 190

Dandy Jim of Caroline, 33, 47
Dixie, 182, 183, 185, 187
Driven from Home, 220
Drunkard's Love Child, The, 220

Early in the Morning, 173

Fine Old Colored Gentleman, The, 184, 209

Going to the Silver Wedding, 33, 66
Grizzly Bear, 190
Gumbo Chaff, 13

Hard Times Come Again No More, 33, 54
Home Again, 86
Hot Time in the Old Town To-night, A, 90, 227
I Hope I Don't Intrude, 33, 56
I Love You in the Same Old Way, 228
I'll Be True to My Honey Boy, 229

Jim Crow, 8, 9, 10, 184
Jim Crow's Polka, 184, 191
Josiphus Orange Blossom, 33, 50

Little Barefoot, 220
Love Among the Roses, 156
Lucy Long, 13

Mary Kelly's Beau, 156
Moriarity, 156
Mulligan Guard, The, 150
My Gal Is a Highborn Lady, 173

Nobody, 173
Not for Joe, 33

Old Clothes Man, The, 16
Old Dan Tucker, 33, 38, 173
Other Side of Jordan, The, 184, 194

Roll Them Roley Boley Eyes, 230
Root, Hog, or Die, 33, 41

Sally, Come Up, 184, 202
Sally in Our Alley, 184
See Me Dance the Polka, 190
Silver Threads Among the Gold, 228
Sittin' on a Rail, 13
Stop Dat Knockin' at My Door, 33, 60
Such a Gettin' Up Stairs, 13, 15

Tassels on Her Boots, 156
That Ain't No Lie, 227
Turkey Trot, 190

Under the Bamboo Tree, 173

Wake Nicodemus, 33, 44
Walk Along, John, 173
Walk in the Parlour, 184, 199
Whistling Coon, The, 169

Yaller Gal That Looked at Me, The, 156

Zip Coon (Turkey in the Straw), 13

"Old-Time Personalities"

Allen, 159
Archer, 14
Arlington, Billy, 148, 154, 161, 180
Arnold, Amos, 167

Arnold, Billy, 70, 167
Arnold, Frank, 167
Backus, 14, 16
Backus, Charlie, 16, 86, 148, 150, 157

INDEX

INDEX

INDEX